Love songs for David Foster from the music industry's brightest stars!

"The first song I ever recorded with David as a producer was 'Somewhere,' from *West Side Story*, and right from the start I was amazed at the way the music just poured out of him. It moved from his mind, to his ears, to his heart—right on down to the tips of his fingers. He made it look easy, which is part of his genius, but the man is meticulous with every note and every phrase, and I love that about him. David, thank you for spending some of your musical life with me. I look forward to working with you again—someday, somehow, somewhere."

—Barbra Streisand

"David Foster came all the way to Quebec to see me in a tent, in the rain, and gave me my first break. Sometimes I don't know if I can reach what he wants, but he's a magician when it comes to vocals. David hears things no other person hears."

—Celine Dion

"Just about everybody in the entertainment business can think back to the one person who gave them their first big break, and for me that person was David Foster. He single-handedly changed my life, and I will never forget it."

—Josh Groban

Turn the page for more acclaim. . . .

"David Foster is one of the most brilliant musical minds of our time, and it has been both an honor and a pleasure to work with him. The man is a force of nature."

—Michael Bublé

"I loved working with David from the first time we were in the studio together. We have worked together on a dozen occasions since, and it is my hope that we never stop making music together."

—Andrea Bocelli

"David Foster combines the creative genius of a great artist, the commercial sense of a strong businessperson, and the generosity of heart of a true philanthropist."

—Edgar Bronfman Jr.

"David Foster has emerged as one of the leaders in the music industry in America, and hence the world."

—Former Canadian prime minister Brian Mulroney

"He's got one of the best ears in the business, this cat does. David Foster can hear an amoeba fart in a typhoon and tell you what key it's in."

—Ronnie Hawkins

"David Foster's music has been the soundtrack of our lives."

—Andre Agassi

HITMAN

Forty Years Making Music,
Topping Charts & Winning Grammys®

DAVID FOSTER
with Pablo F. Fenjves

POCKET BOOKS
New York   London   Toronto   Sydney

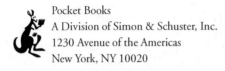

Pocket Books
A Division of Simon & Schuster, Inc.
1230 Avenue of the Americas
New York, NY 10020

First Pocket Books trade paperback edition October 2009

POCKET and colophon are registered trademarks of Simon & Schuster, Inc.

For information about special discounts for bulk purchases,
please contact Simon & Schuster Special Sales at
1-800-506-1949 or business@simonandschuster.com

The Simon & Schuster Speakers Bureau can bring authors
to your live event. For more information or to book an event
contact the Simon & Schuster Speakers Bureau at
1-866-248-3049 or visit our website at www.simonspeakers.com.

Designed by Joy O'Meara

Manufactured in the United States of America

10   9   8   7   6   5   4   3   2   1

The Library of Congress has catalogued the hardcover edition as follows:

Foster, David.
    Hitman : forty years making music, topping charts & winning Grammys / by David Foster.
        p.   cm.
    1. Foster, David.   2. Sound recording executives and producers—Biography.
I. Title.
    ML429.F68A3   2008
    781.64092—dc22
    [B]   2008038405

ISBN 978-1-4391-0306-7
ISBN 978-1-4391-4950-8 (pbk)
ISBN 978-1-4391-6665-9 (ebook)

Contents

1

The Comeback

On a stifling summer day in 1990, I made the long drive from my recording studio in Malibu to Glendale, in the San Fernando Valley. I pulled up in front of a drab building that looked about as impressive as a sheet-metal shop, parked on the street, and approached the unprepossessing entrance. It must have been about ninety degrees out, but it was nice and cool indoors. I signed in at the security desk and took the stairs to the second floor, where an older guy was waiting for me. "You the fella that's here about the Nat King Cole recordings?" he asked.

"That would be me," I said.

He turned and made his way down the corridor, and I followed him through a door and into a huge, musty vault that was stacked with ancient tapes. Most of them were in identical metal cases, piled eight and ten deep in places, and I could make out a number of familiar names on some of the fraying labels: Frank Sinatra, Dean Martin, Peggy Lee, Tony Bennett, Perry Como . . .

We went deeper into the vault. The place looked like that endless government warehouse in the final scene of *Raiders of the Lost Ark*, where the Ark itself—safe inside a sturdy wooden crate—is wheeled to its final resting place among tens of thousands of similar crates.

"Let me think," the old man said, shuffling along and mumbling to himself. "I'm pretty sure I know where it is." He slowed suddenly and I almost bumped into him. "Should be right in this here area somewhere," he said, craning his neck, and I thought he was going to tip over backward. "Yup. There it is."

It was on the second shelf from the top. He reached up and grabbed it and blew the dust off the case, and for a moment a cloud hung in the air between us. He then turned abruptly and I followed him back outside, to the end of the corridor and into a tiny, airless room. He transferred the recording onto a twenty-four-track tape and gave me the copy. I signed for it and thanked him and found my way back into the blazing sunlight, and I climbed into my car for the long return drive to the studio.

I wasn't in a great mood, and I wasn't feeling particularly optimistic about the work that lay ahead. For some time now, I'd been in a bit of a slump, and absolutely nothing was clicking. In previous years, it felt like every single time I wrote a song or produced a song I had a chance at a home run, but that wasn't happening anymore. I wasn't in the Top 40 at the time, and life in the music business is measured by your position on the charts. It was grim. No matter what I did, I couldn't pop the charts. I'd lost my edge, my hunger—whatever the hell you call it.

And it's strange, because over the years, every time I made an album, there was always a point where I would think, *This one's no good. This one's not going to happen.* And I was wrong, of course. Most of my albums had done very well, and some of them had done spectacularly—there were five Grammys sitting on my piano—but where was Number Six? My "sound" had stopped working. I began to wonder whether my career was in the shitter.

Instead of trying to figure out what was wrong, however, to try to fix it, I ran away. I was taking stuff not because it had merit but to keep myself busy, and I was keeping busy because I was trying not to think about the problem. I should have probably gone into therapy, but I didn't want to dig too deep for fear of what I'd find.

This next job seemed unpromising in the extreme: Natalie Cole wanted to sing some classic recordings by her late father, Nat King Cole, to create a string of old standards. But for whom? Did anyone still care about that stuff? The more I thought about it, however, the more it seemed that it might be a good thing for me. This wasn't the type of stuff the radio stations were ever going to play, and at the end of the day that's precisely why I took the job: Because I didn't feel any real pressure to succeed. I hadn't been near the *Billboard* charts in almost two years, and at that point I think I was afraid to even aim for them.

In simple terms, doing Natalie's album was more of the same: I was still running away.

To further complicate matters, I was one of three producers on the project. The others were Tommy LiPuma, an industry veteran, and Andre Fischer, Natalie's then-husband. Some weeks earlier, before I made that drive to Glendale, the three of us met for lunch at Du-par's, a Hollywood restaurant, to divvy up the songs. There were twenty-one of them, and Tommy had written their names on separate scraps of paper, and we went through them one at a time—three kids picking straws. When I saw "Mona Lisa," a song I'd always liked, I snagged it, and when I came across "Unforgettable," Nat King Cole's 1961 classic, I reached for that, too.

"I love that song," I said. "I'll take it."

At that point, I didn't know that Natalie intended to create a duet with her late father. (She only told me about this later, and when she did I thought it was an absolutely brilliant idea.) And in fact, I was kind of surprised that Andre hadn't taken "Unforgettable" for himself. As far as I was concerned, it was the only track on the entire retro album that had half a chance of getting any attention, and surely he'd had the inside scoop on that one.

Lesson #1: *Always go with what you love.*

When I got back to the studio from the vault in Glendale, I handed the tape to David Reitzas, my engineer. He went off to play it for us, and the moment Nat King Cole's voice came over the speakers, filling the room, both of us were completely floored. The quality was beyond anything I had imagined possible. It was just Nat doing vocals—no orchestra, no piano, no nothing—just his crystal-clear, perfectly mellifluous voice. I remember thinking, *Well, if nothing else, we'll be making some beautiful music.*

But I still didn't believe the project was going to do much for Natalie's career—or for mine.

Natalie turned out to be a dream to work with, and an amazing vocalist in her own right. She had been through plenty of crises at that point in her life, including various addictions and the near-drowning of her son, but she was clean and sober and eager to get to work. She'd had a successful career, but it had stalled out—something I could definitely relate to at that point—and she was hoping this was going to turn things around for her. She was also a little worried, wondering whether people would think she was capitalizing on her father's name, but I kept telling her that there was no need for concern. She had lived and breathed that music—it was in her blood—and she needed to keep moving forward. She had every right to pay tribute to the father she loved—and the singer who was loved by us all.

I'd like to tell you that there was a moment when I absolutely *knew* we had a great album on our hands, but that wouldn't be true. I knew it was good, even better than good, but I didn't see it getting any airplay, and I didn't imagine big sales.

I was about as wrong as I'd ever been.

Unforgettable: With Love was a success on every level. The duet became an unexpected Top 10 hit, and the album sold more than eight million copies. It got Record of the Year, Album of the Year, and Natalie took Best Traditional Pop Performance.

And I went home with the Grammy for Producer of the Year.

I remember thinking, *Nobody knows I've been gone, but it sure feels good to be back.*

As I walked off the stage with my Grammys, I remember thinking back to my old friend Ronnie Hawkins, with whom I'd played in Toronto when I was still in my teens. "When it stops happening for you, and you lose your touch, and you're not hitting it dead-on anymore, don't bang your head against a brick wall," he'd advised me. "Retreat and attack from another direction."

That's what I'd done, albeit inadvertently. I'd retreated and attacked from another direction. And damn if it hadn't worked! From that day forward, Ronnie's words became my mantra.

This was a heady period for me, and it was about to get even better—so good, in fact, that it felt almost illegal—but things at home were increasingly difficult. Linda and I were five years into our relationship, and the issues that had plagued us from the beginning—how to manage a blended family—were getting only worse. We were probably in self-denial about the extent of our problems, but at that stage we were still trying to make it work.

At one point, after being locked up in the studio for months, we decided that a change of scenery might help, and we took her two sons, Brandon and Brody, up to Victoria, British Columbia, where I kept my boat. Three days into it, I got a call from Richard Baskin, Barbra Streisand's old beau. "I've got a friend in L.A. who just finished making a movie," Richard said. "He's exhausted, and looking to take a break. He and his wife would love to chill for a couple of days. You'll like them. They're outdoor types. Can you help them out?"

"Sure," I said. I didn't even bother to ask who they were. I wasn't thrilled, though. Linda and I had just had another in a succession of arguments, and I needed a break from my break with Linda, so I turned to her and said, "Why don't you and your boys take the boat for a couple of days, with Richard's friends. I'm sure they're nice people. I'll go chill with my mom."

When Richard called back to tell me that our guests would be Kevin Costner and his then-wife, Cindy, I had a quick change of heart. I wasn't about to leave Linda on my boat with Costner.

On the appointed day, I went to pick up our guests up on the dock, in the dinghy. I hadn't shaved in a few days, and I looked scruffy as hell, and I'm not sure I made a very good first impression. I loaded their bags into the dinghy and then helped them aboard, and we left the dock and made our way into the deep, ominous fog. Cindy later told me that the moment she lost sight of land she was convinced it was all over. "I was sure you were a mass murderer," she said, "and that that was going to be our last day on the planet."

We ended up having a great couple of days with Kevin and Cindy, and Kevin and I discovered that we had plenty in common (or as much as I could have in common with a world-famous heartthrob): We worked in the entertainment world; we knew a lot of the same people; we had to balance career pressures with raising kids; we had a great love of nature; and we were both pursuing our creative dreams.

And it's funny, because not an hour after we lifted anchor, Kevin said, "Man, it would be real nice if we could see some killer whales." And I said, "Well, I've been coming here all my life, and it's a rare occurrence." Not ten minutes later we looked up and saw the biggest pod of killer whales I had ever seen—must have been thirty of them—and we were all completely floored.

As we were getting to know each other, Kevin told me he was thoroughly burned out, having just produced, directed, and starred in a movie that had been five years in the making. "It's a little western," he said. "It's called *Dances with Wolves*. I'd love to invite you and Linda to the premiere."

I didn't think I'd hear from him again—this was Hollywood, after all—but amazingly enough we were invited to the film's star-studded premiere. We sat with Sidney Poitier, Morgan Freeman, and Mel Gibson and his wife, surrounded by other A-list heavyweights, and all of us were completely mesmerized by the three-hour film. I remember thinking, *Holy shit! This guy is a fucking genius!* He was also quietly self-effacing. "*Little western*"? More like *Gone With the Wind*, Part 2.

I figured Kevin was about to make the leap from a sexy dramatic lead—*Silverado, No Way Out, Bull Durham, Field of Dreams*—to the hottest, most bankable triple-threat in town, and I figured right. The Civil War-era epic went home with seven Academy Awards, including Oscars for Best Motion Picture and Best Director of a Motion Picture—not bad for a directing debut!

The next thing I did wasn't exactly a career move, but it was an idea Linda had come up with, and it was close to both our hearts. We got about a hundred people together on the Warner Bros. lot in Burbank to record "Voices That Care," which I'd composed with Peter Cetera, and for which Linda had written the lyrics. This was right after the first Gulf War started, and it was our way of supporting the troops. It wasn't about being for the war, or against it; it was simply our way of letting the men and women on the ground know that we were thinking of them.

The first guy we got to commit was Kevin Costner—I guess I leaned on him a little, having shown him a good time on my boat—and after that it was easy. We got everyone from Meryl Streep and Michelle Pfeiffer to Will Smith and Billy Crystal. I brought Celine Dion down for it, of course, and I had Kenny Rogers there, too, along with Michael Bolton and Kenny G and half the artists I'd worked with over the years. Jeff Wald and Irving Azoff, two terrific managers, were instrumental in helping it come together.

On the day of the actual recording, before we got started, a guy I'd never seen before got up on stage and gave a little speech, talking about what a great project this was, and how much he appreciated being part of it. I thought he was some guy who worked in the recording studio, but it turned out to be the very humble Bob Daly, chairman of Warner Bros. Pictures. He later married my close friend Carole Bayer Sager, and we became good friends.

The event was filmed. We documented everything from the recording of the song to the presentation of the video to the troops, and the show aired on Fox on February 28, 1991, without commercials. We raised more than two million dollars for the Red Cross and the USO.

Some weeks later, Kevin called to tell me he was making a new movie. "I think you should do some of the songs for the soundtrack," he said. "It's called *The Bodyguard.*" The film was based on a Lawrence Kasdan script that had been around for fifteen years. Kevin was starring, with Whitney Houston, and it was being directed by Mick Jackson, a Brit. "You interested?" Kevin asked.

Kevin Costner and Whitney Houston? Are you kidding?

As I started to work on the *Bodyguard* soundtrack, I got a call from Quincy Jones, inviting me to lunch at his house. Quincy had hired me dozens of times as a session musician and was something of a mentor to me, and I can say without reservations that the man is a musical genius. In his incomparable career, he has produced music for Frank Sinatra, Sarah Vaughan, Ella Fitzgerald, Ray Charles, and Michael Jackson, among others, and the man had close to thirty Grammys to show for it. (Michael Jackson's *Thriller* is still the best-selling album of all time, with more than fifty million copies sold.)

Quincy and I had lunch at a very long table, with him at one end and me at the other, and we were forced to speak loudly to make ourselves heard.

"David," he bellowed, "you are about to do the most important project of your life."

I didn't understand what he meant. Maybe he had read the script and thought it would prove explosive. It tells the story of a former Secret Service agent, to be played by Kevin Costner, who is assigned to protect a singing superstar, to be played by Whitney Houston, and how they end up falling in love. Or maybe that wasn't it at all. Maybe he was basing that prediction on the fact that Kevin and Whitney were probably the two hottest commodities in entertainment at the time, and that my involvement with the project would propel me to new heights.

"What do you mean?" I asked.

"You'll see," he said. He smiled from the far end of the table. I still didn't get it. Did the guy have a Third Eye?

When I sat down with the team to discuss the soundtrack, Kevin said he wanted Whitney's big song to be Jimmy Ruffin's 1966 Motown ballad, "What Becomes of the Brokenhearted." I created a demo of the song, written by a trio of Motown songwriters, and worked on it for two days, trying to figure out how it was going to play on screen. Despite the great hook—*What becomes of the brokenhearted / Who had love that's now departed*—none of it really stuck, and it seemed forgettable and a bit depressing. The chorus ends with, *I know I've got to find / Some kind of peace of mind / Maybe*—and that wasn't exactly the feel-good jolt we were looking for. Part of this stems from the fact that some of these older songs don't have much going for them besides the hook. This is because back in those days the songs were two, two and a half minutes long, but in the nineties we were making four-minute tracks, and sometimes the space was hard to fill. It's sort of like what Johnny Carson said when he hosted the 1979 Academy Awards: "Welcome to two hours of sparkling entertainment spread over a four-hour show."

When I finally had a demo, I went to talk to Whitney about it. She was shooting a performance scene at the Mayan Club, in downtown L.A., and when they wrapped we met in her trailer. I played her the demo and she looked at me blankly. I knew what she was saying: She didn't like it. *At all.* "I'm sorry," I said. "I can't get my head around it. And to be completely honest, I don't think it's a good choice."

"You're probably right," she said. "But please go back and try it one more time."

As I worked on the next iteration, I learned that Paul Young, a British pop star, had just finished working on his own version of the song, and that it was moving up the *Billboard* charts. I felt immense relief— I didn't want to work on that damn track—and I immediately called Kevin, trying to hide my joy: "We're fucked, man. Paul Young's done a version of 'Brokenhearted' and it looks as if it's going to be a hit."

Kevin called me back the next day. "I've got the perfect song," he said. "'I Will Always Love You'."

I scanned my memory. "Never heard of it," I said.

"Get a copy and listen to it. It's perfect for my movie."

I went out and found a version by Linda Ronstadt—nowadays, with the Internet, you punch in the name of a song and every iteration pops up, but it wasn't that easy back then—unaware that the song belonged to Dolly Parton, and that it had hit *Billboard*'s country charts in 1974. The heavens split open the moment I played it. I could literally hear the finished Whitney recording in my head—the key change, the rousing strings, the big finish—and I knew *exactly* what I had to do to make it soar. Now I was genuinely excited. I called Kevin with the good news, but suddenly he had more ideas. "By the way, at the opening of the song, I want her to sing a cappella." Instinctively, as a record producer/composer/arranger, this stopped me dead in my tracks. I didn't think Whitney should sing without instrumental backing, not even for the opening. "Kevin, that's a lousy idea. If you want a cappella for the scene in the movie, fine. But for the single record, I'm going to put music around it."

"Just try it," he said.

I went to the studio and did what I'd been asked, giving Kevin a forty-second a cappella opening. I used a terrific singer named Nita Whitaker and we nailed that demo to the cross. The big pause, the boom, the uplifting key change. It really worked. It was one of those soaring moments that make people crazy with emotion, and that's what I look for in designing every single song: One thrilling moment when, if you're playing it live, the audience will jump to its feet and roar.

A couple of nights later, I went to Whitney's dressing room again and played the demo. She absolutely loved it. I mean *loved* it.

When it came to time to shoot the scene that features the song, I was in the ballroom of the Fontainebleau Hilton Resort in Miami, with Kevin and Mick, the director, and they told me they wanted the performance to be real—in other words, no lip-synching. While we were still rehearsing, I got a phone call from Dolly Parton, who had heard that we were using her song in the film. She shared with me a rather significant detail: "By the way," she said, "don't forget there's a third verse that Linda Ronstadt never did on her version."

"What are you talking about? *What* third verse?" I asked.

"There's a third verse. I'll give it to you over the phone."

When I got off the phone, I had to run into the rehearsal and stop everything. "Guys, I just found out about a third verse. We haven't demo'd it. We've got to make the song forty seconds longer." The third verse made so much sense—*And I hope life will treat you kind / And I hope that you have all / That you ever dreamed of*—that we just had to use it.

On the night of the actual shoot, it was pouring rain. Whitney was about ready to step out onto the ballroom stage, and the recording musicians were hidden offstage, waiting for their cue. I had to keep running back and forth to make sure everything was in place, and to repeat, for maybe the tenth time, exactly how I wanted the musicians to play the song.

Kevin wanted it to look absolutely seamless, but recording while filming is never easy to pull off, and I wasn't optimistic. Whitney's first run-through was spectacular, however, and everything fell magically into place. When she opened her mouth, I realized that Kevin Costner had come up with one of the greatest ideas in the history of movie music. Whitney's mom, Cissy Houston, the renowned soul and gospel singer who had recorded with Mahalia Jackson, Aretha Franklin, and Elvis Presley, was standing right beside me in the ballroom, and she realized it, too. At one point, she turned to me and said: "You know, you're witnessing greatness right now." She was right.

Whitney really nailed it.

My recording team and I returned to L.A. to perfect the lead track, as well as some of the other songs we did for the movie, including "I Have Nothing," which I co-wrote with Linda; Aaron Neville's "Even If My Heart Would Break," with Kenny G on sax; and "Run To You."

When Whitney came into the studio to fine-tune some of the vocals, she was a revelation. It had been a bit of a challenge to get her to show up, since she was still busy filming, but once she arrived she'd toss off her jacket, step up to the microphone, and go like a racehorse. And she definitely had that star power thing going on: You could feel she was in the room before you saw her, and you knew she was gone even if you hadn't seen her leave.

With the exception of "I Will Always Love You," we recorded the *Bodyguard* tracks first, and Whitney mimed them brilliantly to a playback on camera for the movie. But she couldn't always do what I asked her to do, and in fact she very rarely gave me *exactly* what I wanted. I'd say, "Whitney, I want you to go"—and then I'd warble some kind of lick, and she'd understand my shorthand and say, "Okay, got it." But then she'd deliver something totally different, and many times it was better than what I thought I was looking for. When it didn't work, however, I would tell her, in my usual blunt manner, and it didn't take her long to realize that I don't believe in compromise.

I had the greatest respect for Whitney, and I believe the feeling was mutual, but we never became close friends. I also liked Bobby Brown, her future husband, who was there all the time. He'd be in the control room with me, egging her on: "Yeah, baby, that's fantastic! It's great. It's unbelievable. You're amazing, baby!"

They were inseparable and fueled each other with their manic energy, and she missed Bobby whenever he left the studio. She worked hard, and was even more focused without him there, but she always had her eye on the phones. Every time they lit up she'd stop singing and go, "Is that my man? Is that my Bobby callin'?"

I didn't see any hint of abuse, or of drugs, but they certainly seemed addicted to each other. They loved each other to a point of serious co-dependency, and when Bobby was gone too long she'd begin to fade. Maybe it was love's version of the shakes.

Over the years, some people have told me that they don't think *The Bodyguard* was Whitney's greatest album, but I believe I pushed Whitney to one of her greatest vocal performances ever, especially on "I Have Nothing."

And the song came about in a funny way. Linda actually wrote the lyric, but Mick Jackson, in his infinite wisdom, thought the sentiments were all wrong, so he made her write an entirely different second lyric. She did, and then together we wrote a third lyric that just ragged on his choice, albeit good-naturedly. (*Take me for all I have / Take my creative lyrics and turn them to crap.*) Luckily, Mick has a solid enough sense of humor; he got the message and we went back to Linda's original lyric.

The song had to be run by Kevin Costner to make sure *he* liked it. (Doing music for films is always by committee, but in this case it was tolerable because I really respected Kevin's opinion.) Again, I asked Nita Whitaker, who had done such a tremendous job on the demo for "I Will Always Love You," to demo this one for me. Because there was no piano in Kevin's office, I asked my friend, Alan Thicke, whom I'd known since my jingle days, if we could use his Toluca Lake home—near the Warners lot, where Kevin had his office—to perform the song, live. We took Nita to Alan's place and met Kevin there. We did the song for him and he flipped for it. He flipped for Nita, too, and ended up putting her in the movie. (She played the act that's on just before Whitney's character performs at the Oscars.)

But the story was far from over.

The soundtrack for *The Bodyguard* was coming out on Arista, the label founded by Clive Davis, one of the industry's premier record executives. He is a brilliant guy with golden ears, but he also had a well-earned reputation for scrutinizing and overanalyzing everybody's music. When the time came to mix the song and send it to him, I knew that he would get back to me with a bunch of comments and suggestions for the remix. Not because the song necessarily needed it, but because he was Clive Davis—and he could.

So I thought I'd outsmart him. I asked my engineer, David Reitzas, to do a passable rough mix. I didn't want him to spend twelve hours on something Clive was going to change anyway.

"Don't waste a lot of time," I said.

Reitzas came up with an impressive mix, but there were a number of things we both wanted to change—the vocal reverb wasn't quite right; the strings weren't loud enough; the sax was *too* loud; we wanted to add a guitar lick near the end—but I messengered the DAT over to Clive's office anyway. (DAT for Digital Audio Tape format, which was state-of-the-art back then; they can be copied and recopied with no degeneration in sound quality.) I knew Clive was going to ask for changes, and by sending him a substandard mix I was simply buying myself time to create the perfect version of the song. I had my own vision for it, and I wasn't going to sell my vision short.

I also planned on doing some additional work on the live ballroom recording. Whitney's vocals were terrific, as I've said, but there were parts of the track that didn't work for me—a direct result of recording and filming simultaneously.

In short order, Clive called with startling news: "I love it!" he said. "I absolutely *love* it." I had never heard Clive Davis say that before, *ever,* and certainly not on a first pass.

"Great, *great,*" I said, but my heart sank. I had more work to do, and I stumbled my way through the rest of the conversation. "Well, Clive, you know, there are just a couple more things I want to do with it to make it tiny little bit better,"

"Sure, okay," he said, "but I *love* this."

Coming from Clive, that was a warning: *Don't mess with it!*

I went back and did what I had to do, a process which took a dozen hours, and sent the remix to Clive. "I made only a few changes," I said. I guess I was relying on the power of suggestion.

But I should have seen what was coming. "What did you do to it?" he said. "I *hate* it. Why did you make all these changes? I *told you* I loved it."

I spent another dozen hours at the board trying to tweak the tweaks, thinking maybe he'd *forget,* but Clive Davis doesn't forget. Two months after the insanity started, we were still arguing. "What are you *doing* to me?" he said. "The original mix was perfect!"

Then we really got into it. "I don't know how you can say that," I said. "It's not there yet. I'm still working on it. I put my heart and soul into that song, and I don't want to use that mix."

And Clive shot back: "You know something, David? I think we should get off the phone before one of us says something he'll regret."

I took a deep breath, braced myself, and came clean: "Clive, I've got to be honest with you. That mix doesn't even exist anymore. That original mix was actually a *rough mix*. We threw it together in twenty minutes. I don't have it."

"But I do!" he said. "I've been carrying it around in my pocket all summer. I'll get it back to you, you'll master it, and that will be the final record."

To this day, I happen to think that my mix was superior. We'll never know, however. We mastered the original DAT and that became the record. The sax remained out of tune and there was no electric guitar tacked onto the end. And the vocals stayed the same.

The song was a history-making blockbuster. "I Will Always Love You" locked in at number one on *Billboard*'s Hot 100 for an astonishing fourteen straight weeks, which at the time was the longest run ever. The soundtrack sold an unprecedented one million units a week for two weeks in a row. The single, by one count, sold some ten million copies worldwide, crossing over from pop, and hit Number One on *Billboard*'s R&B, Adult Contemporary, and radio airplay charts. The film went on to gross $411 million worldwide, and today the soundtrack ranks as one of the all-time top-selling albums in the world, with over forty million units—grossing as much as the film. It was *mind-blowing*.

In the months and years that followed, I often heard "I Will Always Love You" described as "the love song of the century," and I'm not going to argue with that. I'm very proud of it, and proud of having been part of a signature moment in Whitney's career. Whether you loved it or hated it, the song made you *feel*, and at the end of the day that's what it's all about. Whitney's mother had it right: We caught lightning in a bottle that night.

When the Grammys finally rolled around in 1994, all hell broke loose at the awards: "I Will Always Love You" won for Record of the Year, the soundtrack won for Album of the Year, Whitney walked off with Best Female Pop Vocal Performance, and I took home my second

Producer of the Year award in three years. I also won a Grammy for Best Instrumental Arrangement Accompanying Vocals for "When I Fall in Love," which Celine Dion sang as a duet with Clive Griffin. (I had to beat out two of my own nominated tracks to win: "I Have Nothing" and Streisand's "Some Enchanted Evening.") I went up on stage several times to accept our awards, and it was a damn sight more fun than the 1993 Grammys, when I was nominated for seven awards and won nothing.

Before any of this happened, however, while *The Bodyguard* was still grinding its way through production, I went back to work with Celine Dion.

I had introduced her to American audiences with *Unison,* and our next effort was *The Colour of My Love.* The lyrics to the title song— and very few people know this—were written by Dr. Arthur Janov, the Santa Monica-based author of *The Primal Scream.* Art is a friend of mine, and for many years we have been working on a musical, and one of our songs turned out to be perfect for Celine—so we cannibalized our own work. We really didn't want to give it up, though. It was our best song, and we hoped our musical would eventually end up on Broadway, but Celine wanted it so badly that we eventually caved in.

And you know, now that I think about it, I am reminded that the lyrics to another of Celine's songs were written by an even unlikelier guy, my friend Edgar Bronfman, Jr., who was then running Universal. In his other life—his dream life—he was a songwriter, and over the years he had always asked me to think of him if I ever needed a good lyricist. One day, I got a call from Celine's camp, asking me if I'd write a song for her for a Japanese soap opera, and I came up with the melody that very night. Then I remembered what Edgar had said, and I called him at home. "Would you be interested?" I said.

"Yeah," he said. "Absolutely. Send it over."

"Great," I said.

On Monday, bright and early, I called to find out where my lyrics were, and he said he hadn't even had time to start thinking about them.

"But Edgar," I said, "I told you I needed them by Monday."

"No, you didn't," he said. "We just acquired Universal and I have like a thousand things to do. I would have never agreed to this."

"Well, I *thought* I told you I needed them by Monday," I said, ignoring the fact that he had suddenly become the most powerful man in the entertainment business. "How about if I give you till tomorrow? Will that work?"

"Tomorrow?" he said. "That's like a minute from now in my life!"

"Well, I'm sorry," I said. "But I still need it tomorrow."

By that time he was trapped, of course, since in a way he had committed to doing this for me—at least as far as I was concerned. So he stayed up all night and pounded it out, and the lyric was really good. The song is called "To Love You More," and at one point Edgar wrote: *Don't go you will break my heart / She won't love you like I will / I'm the one who'll stay / When she walks away.*

When we went to record the song, he actually came to Los Angeles—to the Record Plant—and the whole thing was surreal. This was the chairman of Universal—movies, music, theme parks, the whole thing—and he was sitting beside me with the lyrics while Celine was rehearsing, making changes as we went along. "Maybe she should say 'it' there instead of 'and'."

I loved it, and Celine loved it. It was a great day. We were in the studio till three in the morning, but it was worth it: That little song ended up selling fifty million copies. It was released in Japan in 1995, in Canada the following year, and in the U.S. a couple of years after that—and it became the most successful song in Edgar Bronfman's career as a lyricist (so far).

Speaking of hits, I actually passed on Celine's biggest song ever,

"My Heart Will Go On"—the title track from the film *Titanic*. To this day I don't relate to that song. I think James Horner is a brilliant composer, but that song just didn't do it for me. I remember trying to talk René out of doing it. "You shouldn't do that song! It's really not that good!" But he didn't listen to me, and he advised Celine to record it.

There's another lesson for you: *If you're gonna go wrong, go wrong big.*

I sure went wrong big on that one. But I dislike the song to this day, and the funny thing is I never stop hearing about it. I'll be on a plane or something, and the person next to me will ask me what I do, and I say I'm a music producer. And then they'll ask me if I've produced anything they might have heard, and I mention a few of the artists I've worked with: Streisand, Whitney, Natalie, blah blah, blah. And whenever I mention Celine, they invariably say the exact same thing. "Oh my God! 'My Heart Will Go On' is my favorite song ever!" Not the guys usually, but all the women under ninety. And I always have to say, "Well, I didn't produce that one." And they don't believe me—at that point they begin to wonder whether I even know Celine, or whether I'm even in the music business. They think I'm bullshitting them because that song *defines* Celine—it's who she *is*.

At that point I have to explain the whole story, why I didn't take it, etc., and it's long and convoluted, so more recently—when people tell me they love that song—I just smile and nod and thank them, and I take credit for it. I feel badly for Walter Afanasieff, who actually produced it, but it's just easier to say I did it because it seems to make people happy. But Afanasieff produced that song with Simon Franglen and James Horner, and they deserve all the credit. Especially Walter: This is a man who started out as Whitney Houston's arranger and went on to produce for Mariah Carey, Lionel Richie, Luther Vandross, Destiny's Child, Christina Aguilera, and for just about every other singing sensation on the planet.

I still get that once a week, though. "Oh I love the *Titanic* song!" And at some point, if I keep lying, I'm going to start believing I actually did produce it.

Still, when I pass on something, I pass big. I passed on *Flashdance*. I thought, *Welder by day, disco dancer by night? Are you fucking kidding me?*

Still, Celine is in a class by herself. People often ask me about her, just as they ask me about the other artists I've worked with, and I can relate to that—I'm curious about famous people, too. And Celine is the one artist I've worked with who should write a book about how to be a perfect artist; and I believe this for two simple reasons. One is that Celine has been a star for so long that she doesn't really know anything else, so she never behaves like a diva. If I ask her to do something, she does it without complaint. "You tell me what to sing," she'll say. "You tell me when I should go loud, soft, up, down, whatever, I'll do it."

And two, Celine is incredibly down-to-earth, a rarity in a star of her magnitude. When we worked on her first album, *Unison,* she would raise her hand and ask permission to go to the bathroom. And when we last worked together, this past year, on an Elvis Presley duet for *American Idol,* she still raised her hand and asked to be excused whenever she left the microphone.

She is humble almost to a fault, unlike many stars, male and female, who are quick to disown the people who helped them scale the heights. I believe they do this because they are trying to distance themselves from their modest beginnings. They don't like to be reminded that that they were once nobodies. Celine is most definitely *not* one of those people.

I also admire Celine because she's smart enough to trust her camp. I tell young artists all the time that they shouldn't change their camp while it's working. She trusts her songwriters, she trusts her arrangers, and she trusts her producers. Most of all she trusts René, who discovered her when she was twelve years old, has managed her career brilliantly, and who many years later ended up marrying her. Their story is truly one of the great love stories of all time. They love each other like no two people I've ever seen.

Funny enough, while I was working on this book, somebody asked me if I had read Celine's book. I didn't realize she'd written a book, or that she'd had several books written about her, but I was informed that in one of them she complained about one of her sessions with me. We were working on "All By Myself," from her 1996 *Falling Into You* album, and apparently I kept making her do the song over and over again. There's a very difficult note in that song, and it's a tough note to hold, but that was also the moment that I had specifically designed to bring a live audience to its feet—the moment that *makes* the song— and that moment hadn't existed in the original version. If I pushed her, that's why I pushed her. Still, that being said, in her book she describes me as being cold and contemptuous that day, and she claims that at one point I said, "I can always ask Whitney to do it." I don't remember saying that, but if I did, I can tell you I was kidding—and it wouldn't be the first time my twisted sense of humor got me in trouble. Anyway, at the end of the day, Celine was right: Her first take was her best, and the other four takes ended up in a vault somewhere, fated never to see the light of day.

While Celine and I were working on "The Power of Love," I was also working at the Record Plant, on a Michael Bolton album. One night Kenny G was in the studio with us, playing sax, and it was getting late. At around midnight I said, "I'm tired. I've got to go home."

But Bolton is very persistent. "Come on, David. Just give me one more hour." He can also be very protective of his voice. On more than one occasion, he'd show up at the studio with a scarf around his throat, pop a couple of throat lozenges, then approach the mike and hum a few bars. "Ugh," he would say. "Not going to happen today. Not feeling anything." And everyone would have to go home. But who are we to argue with that? The man is one of the great vocalists of all time, and if he says it's not going to happen, it's not going to happen.

Finally, at 2:00 a.m., I said I'd had enough, and I got into my Chevy Suburban for the forty-five-minute drive back to Malibu. When I was about ten minutes from home, zipping along the Pacific Coast Highway, I looked up and saw what appeared to be a homeless man standing in the middle of the road in nothing but a pair of shorts. His arms were spread wide, sort of like Jesus.

In the split-second it took me to react, it was already too late, and I hit him dead center at about forty miles an hour. He flew ninety feet and landed in the middle of the road, and I got out of the car in a complete panic. I dialed 9-1-1 on my cell phone. "I've just killed a homeless person," I said, and my voice was at least an octave higher than normal. "Please send help."

I gave the emergency operator my location, and a few details about the accident, and ran off to see if I could help the poor guy. At that point, however, given the impact, and the speed at which I'd been driving, I wasn't really expecting any miracles.

He was lying across the dividing line, in a fetal position, and there was blood everywhere, and he seemed to be trying to lift his hand, so I took his hand and sat next to him and cradled him as best I could. "You're going to be all right," I said, my voice cracking. "They're sending help." But in my heart I knew he was dead. There was no way a human being could have survived that collision.

I'm not sure he was conscious, but I kept talking to him, telling him that help was on the way, and that he was going to be just fine, and then I saw a pair of headlights coming at us through the darkness. Now I thought, *Holy shit! We're both going to get run over!* I stood up and waved frantically until the driver saw me and slowed down. It was a big truck, and we were at the crest of a hill, and fortunately he hadn't been going very fast. When he stopped, I hurried over and literally yanked his door open, still in a panic, and the poor guy—a Hispanic who didn't appear to speak English—must have thought he was in the middle of a horror film. "Man, I need help right now! Come on! Help me take care of this guy! I hit this homeless guy with my truck! I don't think he's going to make it!"

To his credit, he didn't panic or try to run away. He left the truck and followed me back to where the guy was lying, probably dying on me, just as a helicopter roared into view and landed less than fifty yards away, right on PCH. A moment later, two sets of cops arrived in two patrol cars, and I tried to explain what had just happened. I was in shock, only semi-coherent, and then I saw two paramedics hurrying past with a big black body bag and my heart just sank. The guy was gone; I'd killed a man. A moment later, however, I heard the paramedics hollering excitedly. "He's alive!" "Get him in the chopper!" Within a minute, they had him in the helicopter, and seconds later it lifted off and whisked him away.

At that point, still in a daze, I phoned Linda and told her what had happened, and she arrived within five minutes—the accident had occurred that close to home. For the rest of the night, I was practically in a coma, lying there with my eyes open, unable to sleep, unable to move. And every so often I'd be jarred by a violent flashback, where I found myself repeatedly reliving the accident, exactly as it had happened. It was surreal. I thought that kind of thing happened only in the movies.

The next morning it was on the news, and Linda came into my room and said, "David, that homeless guy you hit wasn't a homeless guy. It was Ben Vereen."

"Ben Vereen? How could it be Ben Vereen? I just met Ben Vereen in Canada a few months ago." It was true. I'd done a benefit in Montreal with Celine, and Vereen, an actor/singer/dancer, had been the master of ceremonies.

"Well, the news is saying it's Ben Vereen," Linda said. "They say he's in the intensive-care ward, and it looks like he's not going to make it."

For the next three days, I literally could not get out of bed. I was crushed with depression. I have this saying, "I can only be as happy as my unhappiest child," and at that moment I felt as if Ben Vereen was one of my kids, as if I was somehow responsible for him, and obviously he couldn't have been feeling too happy just then.

I kept trying to get information about Ben's condition, but nobody was able to help. Finally I reached David Loeb, Ben's musical director, and he told me an amazing story. Apparently, earlier that same evening, Ben had been in another accident in which he totaled his Corvette. He had struck his head on the mirror, and his manager had taken him to the hospital, but he refused treatment, so she took him back to her house, in Malibu, and Ben ended up crashing on her couch.

In the middle of the night, Ben woke up in a confused state and decided he would walk the seven miles to his own house. He let himself out of her place in nothing but his shorts, and that's when I hit him—as he was making his way along PCH.

Now here's the most amazing part of the story: When the chopper got him to the hospital, for the second time that evening, he was unconscious and in no position to refuse treatment. The doctors did a complete body scan and found a subdural hematoma in his brain, caused by the earlier accident. If they hadn't found it, he would have bled out in his brain and been dead by 7:00 a.m. In other words, it's a good thing he got out of bed to walk the seven miles home, and it's a good thing I ran him down and put him back in the hospital, where he belonged.

When I was finally sufficiently recovered to get out of bed, I called constantly for updates on Ben's condition, and about ten days later I was told that he was doing much better and would soon be starting rehab. At that point, the fog lifted a bit, and I began slowly going about my normal life. But he was never far from my thoughts. His recovery was my recovery. Until he was well, I wouldn't be well.

I made inquiries about visiting him, and everyone kept putting me off, saying he wasn't ready, but three months after the accident my phone rang early one evening. "Hello?" I said.

"Good hit," a voice said. It was Ben.

Good hit.

2
Perfect Pitch

When I was four years old, as the story goes, my mother was in the living room, dusting the piano, and hit one of the notes. "That's an E!" I called out.

"What did you say?"

"I said, 'That's an E.'"

My mother didn't have a clue about music. I had never once heard her whistle or hum or even make a vague musical sound. She hit the same key again.

"That's the one," I called out. "That's an E."

From the privacy of the utility room, I could hear her picking up the phone and dialing a number. I knew she was calling my father. "Morry," she said. "Listen to this." She hit the note. "Is that an E?" she asked.

My father was quite the musician, but he couldn't tell over the phone, so he came home during his lunch break. The moment he walked in the door, my mother led him to the piano and struck the key again. "Yeah," he said. "That's an E. The boy has perfect pitch."

My family lived on Vancouver Island, British Columbia, and I was the only boy in a family of seven children. My father was a maintenance yard superintendent for a nearby township and never made more than ninety bucks a week. My mother was a homemaker. We had no money, but we weren't poor. I know that sounds like a bit of a cliché, but I can't think of a better way to articulate it. I never felt deprived in any way. Ours was a happy household.

Being the only boy had distinct advantages, not the least of which was that I had my own room. It was the utility room, admittedly, and I slept on a small army cot next to the washer, with my clothes neatly stacked below, but it was *my* room and I was thrilled to be there.

Not long after my father determined that I had perfect pitch, my parents signed me up for piano lessons. I loved every minute of it, but I wasn't wild about practicing. One day, for no apparent reason, I absolutely refused to put in my twenty minutes, so my mother made me sit at the piano till midnight. She wasn't musical, but she understood that I was, and she wanted me to develop my talent. She taught me not to take it for granted.

She was a real stickler for rules, my mother, and there were a lot of rules in our house. One of these was that we had dinner at 5:30 every evening, and we weren't allowed to talk unless one of our parents addressed us directly. That might seem a little rigid, but in retrospect I think it made perfect sense: Six girls talking at the same time would have been complete chaos.

Another rule was that we had to go to church every Sunday. My father took us—he sometimes played the organ there—but my mother never went. She used to say that that hour and a half alone in the house, without all eight of us underfoot, was her own special way of going to church, and we never questioned it.

When we got home, I'd change into my regular clothes and do my chores. I'd help my father mow the lawn or stack wood for our wood-burning furnace, and if my room was tidy I was free to hop on my bike and go play with my friends. Nobody worried about safety helmets, or about possible kidnappings, or about drunk drivers; my one responsibility was to listen for my father's familiar whistle, calling me to dinner.

By the time I was six or seven, while I was still working on the foundations of classical music, my father decided to broaden my horizons. Years earlier, before I'd come along, he had played with a local dance band, and he decided to teach me to play barroom-style piano and to sing harmony. "Listen to this, boy," he'd say, and he'd plunge in. "This is a little song called 'Dream a Little Dream of Me.'" I'd sit on the piano bench next to him, watching him play it two or three times, and then I'd play it back to him just the way he'd played it. I think this made him very happy. I'd inherited his talent. "That was pretty good, boy," he'd say. "Now try it this way."

My father also loved making home movies, and I think he had real talent as a filmmaker. He had an eight-millimeter camera, and he did close-ups and two-shots and reverse-angles, all of it instinctively. He did special effects, too. If it was my birthday, for example, he'd make me write on our little blackboard, one letter at a time: "Hi, I'm David. Age 7." And he would shoot two or three frames of each letter so that they would pop up on the screen when he showed the movie, bing-bing-bing-bing-bing. Or "Merry Christmas from the Fosters, 1966," one letter at a time.

He had a very primitive editing machine in the basement, with a small viewfinder, and he'd move the film along, one frame at a time, and use a razor blade to make the cuts. He was absolutely tireless. He chronicled the lives of every one of his seven children, from birth to the day each of us left the nest, and amassed hundreds of hours of home movies of every single one of us, at every age. It was an incredibly labor-intensive hobby. Nowadays, you shoot three hours of video to get three usable minutes, but back then every frame counted. And it was expensive, too. My mother managed the family money, and every two weeks she would give my father only fifteen bucks out of his own paycheck, to spend on cigarettes and coffee, and every two weeks, without fail, he would spend almost a third of it on fifty feet of eight-millimeter film. And of course it was all about us, the kids. I don't think there was a better way than that to show us he loved us. If he had left each of us a million dollars instead of those films, it wouldn't have meant nearly as much.

When I think back on it, it occurs to me that my parents raised me to believe I was truly special. I'm sure the home movies were part of it, just as the music was part of it, but it went deeper than that. Way back when I was five or six, I was somehow made to feel that I was going to do something important in my life. Two or three times a week, at bedtime, my father would visit each of us kids and lie down with us for a few minutes. He wouldn't say much, because neither he nor my mother were particularly communicative, but it was his way of letting us know that he was there. I remember one night in particular, when I asked him, "Do you think I'm gonna live to be old?" And he said, "I *more* than think it. I promise you, you're gonna live to a ripe old age."

I clung to those words as though he had control of my destiny.

Other nights, while he lay next to me, my father would teach me to sing harmony. They were silly little songs like "You Are My Sunshine" or "She'll be Comin' 'Round the Mountain," but I loved every minute of his company. Forty years since his passing, I still miss him every day. I wonder if that's the way it is for everyone.

My mother, Eleanor, was amazing, too. She was up till midnight almost every night, sewing our clothes, down to the coats we wore, and she was up at 6:30 every morning, scrubbing and washing the kitchen floor. I'm not sure we appreciated everything she did for us, but I'm not sure kids ever do.

And it's interesting, because she actually came from a sort of dysfunctional family. Her mother apparently suffered from depression, though they probably didn't call it that back in those days, and Eleanor had three brothers and a father who didn't help much around the house. So from the time she was maybe twelve yeas old she did everything for them: shopping, cooking, cleaning. She was the guardian and the keeper of the castle. And when she began raising a family of her own, she was determined not to have that kind of life, so she turned our home into the classic household: My father earned the money, and my mother took care of everything else. She made sure that everybody got to school on time. She prepared all our lunches. She made the meals every night. She ran the house. And at the end of the day she was the one who made sure we behaved. She did a good job across the board, but especially on that last point. We turned out to be pretty good kids, and the family was always getting invited to the homes of friends and neighbors. When you consider that there were nine of us, that's quite a challenge. Who wants to feed and entertain nine Fosters? But people did, and that's a testament to my mother. She raised seven kids whose company people seemed to enjoy, kids who never got into trouble.

Well, *never* is a strong word. There was one incident when I was ten years old that haunts me to this day. I was out riding my bike with a friend when a policeman drove past in the opposite direction, and I guess I was feeling kind of tough because I turned around and called him a pig.

The officer stopped his car and backed up, tires squealing, and I was too scared to run away. "What did you just call me?" he asked.

"N-nothing," I said. "I didn't say anything."

"Yes you did," he said. "You called me a 'pig'."

"No I didn't," I lied.

"We'll see about that," he said. "We're going back to your house to talk to your father."

He loaded my bike into the car and drove me home, and my father came outside to see what all the fuss was about. "Your son called me a pig," the officer told him.

My father looked at me. "Is that true, boy?" He never once called me by name. He always called me "boy."

And I lied through my teeth. "No," I said. "It is absolutely not true."

My father turned back to the policeman, took a moment, and said, "My son tells the truth. If he says it didn't happen, it didn't happen."

The officer looked at me with disgust, then turned and walked off and climbed into his patrol car and drove away. My father never said another word about the incident, but it has stayed with me my whole life. I had lied to my father, and I felt terrible about it, and after that I tried to keep my lies to a minimum.

By the time I was ten I was a pretty accomplished classical pianist. I loved playing—I wasn't one of those kids who said, "Oh God! Not piano again!"—but I was still pretty lazy about practicing. If I had practiced more, I might have become a serious classical pianist, though probably not a great one. It's likely I would have managed to eke out a living for the rest of my life, but it would have been a life of struggle and obscurity. In that sense, then, I guess it's a good thing I didn't practice much. Still, when all is said and done, I know I owe much of my success to my classical foundation, and I can't stress that enough. I had the same classical piano teacher for six years, Catherine Dash, and I used to ride my bike to her house every Saturday morning. I didn't practice much, and she knew it, but she also knew I had talent, so she didn't bust me over it.

By the time I was eleven, I was getting seriously interested in other types of music—thanks largely to my sisters Ruth and Jeanie, who had part-time jobs at a local coffee shop. From time to time the guy who owned the place would put new 45s in the jukebox and send them home with the old ones. One of the first records I remember hearing was "A Wonderful Time Up There," by Pat Boone. Another was "Mule Skinner Blues," by the Fendermen. I played those two songs to death. I also began watching *American Bandstand,* with Dick Clark, thanks to another sister, Maureen, who would park herself in front of the TV every Saturday morning to watch the show.

I remember being particularly impressed by Paul Revere and the Raiders. I loved their music, but I think I liked their outfits even more.

Another big influence in my musical evolution, aside from my father, of course, was my band teacher at Lansdown Junior High, Bob Bergeson, who allowed me to switch instruments every three or four months, which really helped me grow as a musician. I would play trombone for three months, then I'd play trumpet for three months, followed by tuba and clarinet and bassoon. I never got very good at any of them, but it gave me a working knowledge of every instrument. I used to think Mr. Bergeson was a real pushover—that I was having my way. I'd get bored and ask him if I could try something else, to mix things up, and he always said yes, and it was only years later that I realized it had all been part of his master plan: He wanted me to familiarize myself with as many instruments as possible, and he wanted me to think it was all my idea.

"Having perfect pitch doesn't mean you're a musical genius," Mr. Bergeson once told me. "It's a gift. It means you've got something going on, musically, but if you want to be great you're going to have to work at it."

That was about as pushy as he ever got, and he only got pushy because he knew I was lazy. I only worked hard enough to be better than everyone else, and I think he was trying to tell me that that might not be enough.

Years later, whenever people would ask me to describe perfect pitch, I always had the same answer: "Most musicians are color-blind; I see in color." When I hear red, I know it's red, and even if it's only *minimally* out of tune, if the color's just a tiny bit off, I want to go back and make it perfect. The majority of musicians probably wouldn't notice— if this was math, we'd be talking about fractions of fractions—but my inclination is to go back, redo it, and get it exactly right, and that has turned out to be both a blessing and a curse.

From time to time, after school, Mr. Bergeson and I would go into the empty gym together and jam a little, just the two of us. He wasn't a great sax player, but we were making music together, and I was playing with an adult, and that made me think I might actually have a shot at music as a career. I'd leave the school walking on air, full of hope, and after dinner, if my father was in the mood, I'd jam some more with him.

I was never too tired for music. There was no such thing as too much music.

When I was about twelve, I put a band together, made up of some of the more talented musicians in town, all of whom were older than me. We called ourselves the Starbright Combo and played mostly dance music, and it was pretty much my show. My friend Chris Earthy helped, but I ran the rehearsals, booked the gigs, kept the books, and chose all the music. I even arranged for us to wear matching blazers— not up to Paul Revere standards, certainly, but I do believe we were the hottest thing in Victoria. I was pushy, and maybe a little abrasive at times, but my talent was persuasive. These guys wanted to play with me, even if it meant having my parents drive to their homes and bring them back to our house.

In many ways, music saved me, because I honestly hated school. I didn't like being stuck in class, I didn't like studying, and for two years in junior high there was this kid, Gary Druce, who went out of his way to torment me every day after P.E. He'd towel-whip me and push me around, and he enjoyed making fun of my clothes and my battered Hush Puppies. The Hush Puppies were very comfortable, but I longed for a pair of hip, pointy shoes—winklepickers, we called them. At one point, I actually bought a pair from one of my classmates, but I knew my mother wouldn't approve, so I hid them in the bushes near school and changed into them on my way to class.

By the time I was thirteen, I was making more money than my Dad. It was kind of crazy. I'd book a wedding, say, and I'd ride my bike over to the bride's home to make arrangements with the parents, and when they opened the door they'd find me standing there, a painfully skinny kid with lots of zits.

"Who are you?"

"I'm David Foster. From the Starbright Combo. I'm here about the financial arrangements."

When I got home, I always gave the money to my mother, for safekeeping, and she would leave it on her dresser. Sometimes, if the family was a little short, she might borrow twenty bucks to spend on groceries, but she always paid me back. One of my great regrets is that I didn't just give her the money. I never thought to say, "You don't need to *borrow* it, Mom. Just take it. I'm not even using it." It never occurred to me that my parents could have used a little extra cash—we tend not to see our parents as needy, no matter what the circumstances.

One day, still at age thirteen, I heard the Beatles on the radio. They were playing "She Loves You," and it completely changed my world. I was hooked. I had never heard anything like that in my entire life. It was so foreign-sounding that I was utterly and completely intoxicated by the song, start to finish. I wanted to drop everything and play only that type of music. I pushed the Starbright Combo to become more adventurous, but the locals mostly wanted dance music, so nothing much came of it.

That same year, I got a scholarship to attend the University of Washington's summer music program. This was thanks largely to Dave Dunnet, a band leader at a neighboring school, who had watched me evolve over the years—had watched me win every single talent contest on the island—and had taken great interest in me. He put me on the list for a scholarship, and he was as excited as I was when I got accepted.

My parents drove me to Seattle and left me there, and shortly after they took off, while I was in my dorm room, unpacking, I heard a commotion outside. I went to the window and looked down and saw several police cars and an ambulance out front. One of the students had just taken his life by jumping from the roof.

Despite that inauspicious beginning, I loved the program. I was the youngest kid there—all of the others were high school and college students—and I was impressed by the more talented ones, but I also knew I could hold my own.

One day, Mr. Dunnet came to visit. He was in Seattle to listen to Oscar Peterson play at a local club. I was of course familiar with Oscar Peterson, and a huge fan, but kids weren't allowed in the club, so he couldn't take me. "Is there anything I can bring back for you?" he asked.

"Yes," I said. "Bring me his autograph."

The next morning, before Mr. Dunnet returned to Victoria, he stopped by the campus with Oscar Peterson's autograph. It was written in a beautiful hand, on a large, crisp sheet of paper, and it said, "Dear David Foster, keep working on your music. It's a worthwhile endeavor. Sincerely, Oscar Peterson."

I kept that note in my wallet for twenty years, and some years ago I found myself at a black-tie event with Oscar, and I told him the story about the autograph. And he said, "Oh yeah, kid! I remember that!" I knew he was bullshitting, but he kept the dream alive, and I'm sure he felt good at that moment—knowing he had influenced my career in such a positive and dramatic way.

When I returned home from the summer music program, I came under the influence of our band's bass player, Rick Reynolds, who was a jazz fanatic. He was a decade older than me, and already married, and every Saturday morning he'd fetch me at my place and drive me back to his house to play records for me: Miles Davis. Bill Evans. Herbie Hancock. Count Basie. Horace Silver. Vince Guaraldi. Absolutely everything. Sometimes he played me stuff I hated—Denny Zeitlin, for example, a San Francisco psychiatrist who was also an accomplished avant-garde jazz pianist—and he'd make me suffer through it more than once. "No, no, no," he'd say. "You've got to listen to it again."

When the torture ended, he'd put the record away, very carefully, and return with something else. And when he took the record out of its sleeve, it was like he was holding a baby. He would slip it out very gently, dust it off with a special cloth, and set it on the record player like he was handling plutonium. "Now watch this," he'd say, and he'd reach over and delicately set the needle at the beginning of the recording. "This is Thelonius Monk," he would say. "Wait till you hear this! This is some crazy shit!"

Rick only ever played instrumentals for me. I never heard Billie Holiday or Ella Fitzgerald or Dinah Washington. He just wasn't into vocals. But he gave me a hell of a jazz education, and I really owe him a lot. I had never heard of any of those people because I was raised on an island, and until I was thirteen I didn't even know that there was an actual city with an actual downtown only six miles from our home. Not that it would have made any difference, however, since this was the kind of music known only to true audiophiles. Rick had to send away for every single one of his records, and sometimes it took three months for them to arrive. Whenever a new album showed up, Rick would practically shake with excitement. "You're not going to believe what came in the mail last night," he would tell me.

"What?"

"You'll find out Saturday."

Eventually, with the money I was earning from the gigs, Rick told me where to buy records—this was in the pre-Amazon days—and I began to put together a small collection of my own. At our house, the record player was upstairs, and the piano was in the basement, and I'd play a track—something by Bill Evans, say—then run down to the basement and try to copy it note for note. (That's a big part of learning, by the way: You copy enough musicians and, with a little luck, you eventually develop a style of your own.) After a few months of running up and down the stairs, I was finding it pretty exhausting, and I convinced my father to let me wire an extra speaker and set it in the basement, near the piano. That worked out great. Now I only had to run upstairs to change records.

Rick Reynolds was such a big influence in my life that many years later, when I was in Victoria for a function, I asked him to join me on stage with several of the people who had contributed so much to my musical awakening during those critical early years. They included Catherine Dash, Bob Bergeson, Jo Sargent, and Dave Dunnet, all of whom got a copy of one of my recent platinum albums. I gave a little speech about how much each of them had meant to me, and how important it was for parents to push their kids a little if they had any musical talent at all. "Not to the point where they begin to hate it," I said, "but just inside of that." While I was up there on the stage with them, making my little speech, I remember thinking, *I wish my father could have been here.*

During those early years, our little band was getting pretty well known in and around Victoria, which isn't saying much, but it kept us busy, and it kept me out of trouble. Then I discovered women, and I finally understood what all the fuss was about. I had a couple of girl-friends, and at sixteen I fell in love with a girl in the class behind me. I had met her a couple of years earlier, but I'd always assumed, wrongly, that she was too beautiful for me, and the day she agreed to go out with me was the day I became a hopeless romantic.

Music still came first, however, and before long—after having played with half a dozen different bands—I became part of a very promising group known as The Strangers. We all felt we were so good that we began talking about moving to London, which back then, in the mid-sixties, seemed to be the center of the universe, musically speaking. One day we just decided to stop talking about it and do it. This was easy for the other guys because they were older—some of them were married, with kids even—but I had to get permission from my parents, which actually turned out be a lot easier than I'd expected. My parents were not particularly emotional people. They were even-tempered, almost phlegmatic, and not fond of confrontation. And sure, they had some concerns—the fact that I was dropping out of high school, money, living arrangements overseas—but I had an an-swer for everything. I'd finish school when I got back; the band was really very talented—I could almost guarantee that we'd make money; the lead singer had relatives north of London where all seven of us could crash; etc. To this day I still can't believe that they let me go. They must have had tremendous faith in my talent.

A week before I left, my parents drove me to a music store in down-town Victoria, and, in an act of incomprehensible generosity, took their entire life savings—seventeen hundred dollars—and bought me an electric piano and an amplifier. I learned later that this had put quite a strain on the marriage. My father was old-fashioned, and he felt that a man needed to make his own way in the world, but my mother fought him on this, arguing that as the only son I was entitled to anything and everything they could provide for me. He didn't like that, either. He thought all his kids should be treated equally. (And by the way, these many years later, I agree with him.)

That September, just as my former fellow students were returning to school, my parents put me on the overnight ferry to Vancouver, and the following morning I was on a train to Gander, Newfoundland, with my new piano, my new amplifier, and my six bandmates. One of them had figured out that the cheapest flight to London left from Newfoundland, so we took the train to Gander—a harrowing *nine-day* ride—which turned out to be a truly insane experience. After four days of sitting, numb with back pain and exhaustion, Rich England, the saxophone player suggested that we spend an extra two dollars on a berth, which we could share. Unfortunately, the berth was incredibly narrow, and Rich was a pretty big guy, so I went back to my seat—and he slept like a baby for the next four nights.

When we arrived in London, we made our way to Northampton and crashed with the singer's relatives. The first two months were a complete nightmare. We had arrived with very little money, thinking we were the shit, and we spent weeks going from one club to the next, trying to get hired. Absolutely nothing happened. Nobody even wanted to hear us audition. We eventually found our way to the Roy Tempest Agency, having heard that they were looking for a backup band to work with American artists, most of whom came to London without their regular musicians, and they got us our very first gig— with the legendary Chuck Berry, whom I'd never even heard of. He was supposed to be the Holy Grail of rock and roll, maybe even one of its *inventors,* but I didn't like him and I didn't like his music. That first night, before we went on stage, he didn't even say hello to us. Not a word. And when it was time to play, he followed us onto the stage, plugged in his guitar, and said, simply, "Ready? Let's go." That was all he ever said to any of us. He had no regard for musicians, but the fans loved him.

After the show, some of the more marginal types would come backstage and break out the drugs. I was probably the only person in the room not smoking dope or snorting coke or shooting up, and it really didn't faze me because I already knew that I was never going to do drugs. I don't know when I knew it, or how, or why, but I think a big part of it is the way I was raised. It just never entered my head to do something so self-destructive, and seeing those people—being loud and ridiculous and out of control—only strengthened my resolve. I was not going to let drugs define my career. I was there for the music.

We had one magical moment with Chuck Berry, but it had nothing to do with him. We were about a week into our gig, playing at the Saville Theatre, when I looked up and saw all four Beatles in a private box, wearing their Sgt. Pepper outfits. I couldn't believe it! I tried to say something to Chuck Berry, to share my excitement, but he didn't give a damn, and he still wasn't talking to any of us. "Ready?" he barked. "Let's go."

One night the fans went crazy. I never understood exactly what happened—it was the mods versus the rockers, I guess—but things quickly got out of control. At one point, a fire extinguisher landed on the stage and rolled right between my legs, and we stopped playing and went home. Chuck Berry didn't care, just so long as he got paid.

We also played with Bo Diddley, another blues and rock and roll legend. Unlike Berry, he was a good guy, and I actually learned a valuable lesson from him during the short time we were together. Up until that point, I had never really connected with the rest of the guys in the band. We were playing, and we were playing well, but we weren't *listening* to each other. The bass player wasn't listening to the drummer and the drummer wasn't listening to the guitar player and the guitar player wasn't listening to me. And Bo Diddley taught me that the members of a band have to play as if they are one person. He had the power to make it happen, too. When Bo Diddley came out on stage with his rectangular guitar, he took us to a place none of us had ever been before—he made us *groove*. It was like having sex (or what I thought sex must have been like). Seriously. It was that good. We were really rockin'. And it was something completely *new*. By that point, I'd been exposed to classical music, dance music, American songbook standards, and jazz, and there I was, learning all about rock 'n' roll.

A few weeks into it, the band found a six-bedroom flat in the Earl's Court section of London, closer to the action, and I thought we were in it for the long haul. But one night, two days before Christmas, the guys told me they were going back to Victoria. We had been in London for three months, and all of them were homesick. They missed their kids and their wives and girlfriends, they said, and they were ready to go home.

"We just got here!" I said. "We're going to be famous! This is London! This is Carnaby Street! It's *the Beatles*! This is the shit! You can't go home!"

But they could go home, and they did, and for the first few days I think I was in shock. I kept wondering how they could have left. I couldn't get my mind around the fact that they would quit when I was absolutely convinced that we were on the verge of breaking out.

The winter that followed turned into the most miserable period of my life. I found a tiny little apartment, with a bathroom down the hall that had this machine in it called a shilling meter. If you wanted hot water for your shower, you had to feed money into the machine—and even then the water was tepid at best. I learned how to wire the machine so that I didn't have to pay for the tepid water, and that helped me save money, but it didn't do much to lift my spirits. I didn't know anybody in London, and I couldn't find any work, and I spent most of the day in the flat with only my electric piano to keep me company. It was a period of unrelenting, crushing loneliness. I don't think too many people understand what it's like to go for weeks on end without talking to a soul.

I didn't meet anyone, either. I didn't see anyone in my apartment building, and when I was out in the street I tried to smile at people and make friends, but no one so much as smiled back.

To compound matters, I was slowly but surely running out of money. I went to audition for rock bands and for a children's television show and even tried to sell myself as a piano teacher, but nothing worked—I couldn't get arrested. Most days I just sat in the apartment alone, with my electric piano, and practiced to pass the time. And at four o'clock every afternoon, when I couldn't take it anymore, I'd go out and get my first meal of the day—a Wimpy Burger, for nineteen pence. And once a week, usually on Sundays, I'd treat myself to a baked potato with a side of broccoli. I know it sounds pathetic, but it's the truth. I was lonely, but I wasn't depressed. I really believed that good things were just around the corner. I didn't know how near or far that corner was, but I knew it was there. Still, there were moments of doubt and pain, and sometimes I'd lay awake at night wondering whether I'd ever really make it in the music business.

After three months of this torture, I finally decided I couldn't take it anymore. I wasn't going to spend another miserable week in this miserable, godforsaken city. Unfortunately, by that time I didn't even have enough money for a cheap flight home, and I had to write my parents. I felt awful. They had spent their life savings to buy me an electric piano and an amplifier, and I was returning home with my tail between my legs.

"I'm sorry about this," I wrote. "I just can't do it anymore. I need money for a ticket, and I promise I won't bug you anymore."

My father was not a particularly emotional guy. Or maybe he was, but he didn't show it. The money arrived about a week later—they wired it, without a note or anything—and I booked a ticket for seven o'clock the following morning. A little after four, I went out for a final Wimpy Burger and brought it back to the apartment. I ate it, alone, but I was feeling pretty good. I was going home. I wouldn't be lonely anymore. I'd be with my family and the band would get back together and I'd get to see my girlfriend again.

At around six o'clock, just as I was getting done packing up my gear, somebody buzzed the apartment from out front. I made my way down the corridor to see who it was, and when I opened the door I saw a burgundy Rolls-Royce parked at the curb. There was a driver standing next to the Rolls-Royce, and I saw the vague outlines of a man in the back seat. Then I noticed a guy standing just to one side of the door, looking at me. He was in a crushed-velvet suit that was the same color as the Rolls-Royce, and I recognized him right away. "Are you David Foster?" he said.

"Yes," I said.

"I'm Cat Stevens," he said. "Can I talk to you for a minute? I hear you're a really good keyboard player."

I thought I was dreaming. This was *almost* the equivalent of one of the Beatles showing up at my door. I took him back to the apartment. "Who told you I was a good keyboard player?" I asked.

"Bobby," he said. Bobby Faulds was the lead singer in our now-defunct band. I had no idea that Bobby knew Cat Stevens, or how, or why. "I'm looking for a keyboard player to tour with me for a year. Can I hear you play?"

My heart was really pounding now. I went and took the cover off the piano and plugged in the amp, and for the next nine hours we stood in that shabby apartment and jammed. He hadn't brought his guitar. He was just singing. We did Beatles songs. I played chords. We made stuff up. We were laughing and having a good time.

At around three in the morning, he turned to me and said, "I've been looking for a guy like you for a long time. I want you in my life. I want you to come on the road with me."

I was stunned. Near shock, really. And I couldn't quite believe the words that came out of my mouth. "I have waited a long time to meet someone like you, too," I said. "But I'm really homesick, and in a few hours I'm going to be on a plane on my way back to Canada."

It was almost tragic. It was one of those moments you dream about, and now that it was finally happening I didn't have the energy to take advantage of it.

"I can't talk you out of it?" he said.

"No."

"It'll be good fun," he said. "Good money, too."

"No," I said. "I'm sorry."

A few hours later, I was on an Air Canada plane, on my way home, and I began to wonder what would have happened if I had gone with him. I could have called my parents and said, "You know what? I don't need any money. Everything's cool. I'm going on the road with Cat Stevens." But the fact is, I was so homesick I couldn't do it, even if it meant missing one of the biggest opportunities of my life. And I think at that point I realized that the things you say no to in life are just as important, if not more important, than the things you say yes to. That's another valuable lesson, and I'm glad I learned it early.

In the middle of the flight, I found myself in the plane's tiny bathroom, staring at my reflection in the mirror. It was a little startling. I had left home with a brush-cut and a button-down shirt, and now my hair was almost to my shoulders, and I was wearing this loud, silk shirt that would be an embarrassment to me today.

My parents met me at the airport, and I think they were happy to see me, though it was always hard to tell with them. My father was not too happy about my hair, however.

"Boy," he said, "I can't ask you to cut your hair, and I *won't* ask you to cut your hair, but I need to inform you that you are never to come to my office."

It seemed like a reasonable request.

That night, I hooked up with my old girlfriend—she liked the new 'do—and before long I was playing with some of my former band-mates. I also registered at a local night school—a misnomer, since they held classes during the day—and settled into a pleasant routine. In the morning, I went to class to try to get my high school diploma. And at night, five nights a week, the band played at the Old Forge, a local club. Most nights we stayed after the show and jammed till five in the morning.

At one point, the owner of a local bar/restaurant heard me play and hired me to work for him. Since I was underage, however, I couldn't play in the bar, and he ended up tearing a hole in the wall so the patrons could hear me in both places. I had a very full life: School in the morning, the bar/restaurant from five to nine, five nights a week, and the Old Forge from ten till dawn Tuesday through Saturday.

My parents didn't know what to make of me. I was eighteen years old and I was leading a completely independent life, but I was still living at home, and as far as they were concerned I was still a kid. I had a feeling that one or the other of them always waited up till I got home, to make sure I was safe, and one morning, shortly before dawn, my suspicions were confirmed. I rolled into the house after another all-night jam session, and found my father waiting for me in the living room.

"Hello, boy," he said. He said it calmly, his voice flat and unemotional.

"I'm sorry it's so late," I said.

"Why don't you sit down?" he said.

I figured he was going to give me all sorts of shit about my lifestyle, and about being up till all hours, and about the importance of paying attention at school so that I could get a high school diploma, and I tried hard to look contrite. "I hope you and Mom haven't been waiting up for me," I said.

He didn't say anything. I sat on the couch across from him and it occurred to me that I'd never had a real, adult conversation with my father, that we'd never really talked about anything at all—outside of my chores or my report card or, more recently, about the fact that he was embarrassed by the length of my hair. Our relationship was extreme in its simplicity: He was the adult, and I was the kid.

"So you've been out playing music again, eh?" he said.

"Uh-huh," I said. I was worried about what he was going to say. I was out jamming every night, and I never got home before the crack of dawn, and I was sure he thought I was up to no good. I wondered if I should have made an effort to set them straight—maybe they needed to hear me say that I was an abnormally normal eighteen-year-old boy who didn't drink, didn't do drugs, and had little interest in anything beyond music.

"And you really think you want to be in the music business?" my father said.

"Yeah," I said. "I do. I really do. I really think I can amount to something. Maybe I'll go to Vancouver and get a job in a club. I love music more than anything."

And he said, "You know, from what I've heard, and from the little I know, it sounds like a very difficult business."

"I don't know," I said. "It doesn't seem difficult to me. Everything about it seems just right to me."

It was really strange. Almost surreal. For the first time in my life, I felt he was addressing me as an equal.

"Well, then," he said after a pause. "If that's the way you feel about it, you should probably go for it."

Then he stood up and went off to get ready for work, and I went to my room to try to get a few hours of sleep before night school.

On May 31, 1968, not three weeks after that conversation, my father had a fatal heart attack. I couldn't believe he was gone. I thought back to our final conversation—our one adult conversation—and about how close I had come to never having it at all.

"If that's the way you feel about it," he had said, "you should probably go for it."

My father had given me his blessing to pursue my dream.

3

"Wildflower"

Not long after my father passed away, my girlfriend got an office job in Edmonton, Alberta, about eight hundred miles away, and I decided to follow her east. As it happened, I knew about this guy in Edmonton, Tommy Banks, who was a world-class piano player—and totally plugged into the city. He was an arranger, a writer, and he owned a nightclub and years later he actually went into politics and became a senator, but back then, in 1969, he was looking to leave the band to become part of a jazz trio. I learned this from Mark Vasey, an old trumpet-playing friend from Victoria, who put me in touch with one of the guys in the band. "I know you don't know me," I told the guy, "but I really want that gig, and I was wondering if you'd do me a big favor. Would you put a tape recorder under Tommy's piano to-night, tape the entire evening, and send me the tape?"

"Okay," the guy said. "I'll do it."

As promised, he recorded the entire performance, and he sent me the tape, and I spent an entire week learning every single nuance of every single song, note for note, exactly the way Tommy Banks played it. And when I went to audition for the slot, a couple of weeks later, I had it down cold, and of course I got the job.

I moved to Edmonton and found an inexpensive apartment, and I tried to cozy up to my girlfriend, but she didn't seem too happy to have me back in her life. Still, I didn't let it bother me. I figured it would pass. My life was perfect: I had a perfect job, I had a perfect apartment, and my girlfriend just needed a little time to adjust before she realized that she was still desperately in love with me.

But one day she walked into my apartment and said, "I have a new boyfriend. I don't want to be with you anymore." It was brutal. I mean, I'd had my share of heartache in my eighteen years, but nothing like that. I was devastated.

I still had a great job, though, and I concentrated on my music. I also began dating indiscriminately. I remember sitting around the club with the guys one night, talking to three girls, and one of them said something about flying. "I'm a pilot," I said. I wasn't a pilot at all, of course, but I'd always been interested in planes—an interest I'd shared with my father—and suddenly the girl next to her said, "Great! Maybe you can take us flying some weekend." And I said, "Sure, no problem." And the third girl said, "How about this weekend?"

I made up some lame excuse about my crazy schedule, and the next morning, bright and early, I went over to the Edmonton Flying Club and signed up for lessons, and twenty-nine days later I had my license. I took lessons during the day, every day, and at night I worked at the club, and my instructor told me he had never met anyone who was so committed to becoming a pilot, and who had managed to do it so quickly. I had my reasons, of course. Four weekends later, I had those girls in the plane with me—and I got results.

Another time I went flying with a couple of the guys in the band. We had been playing music in some town in northern Alberta, way up near the Arctic Circle—Yellowknife, I think it was—and the following morning we went to a local airfield and I rented a small plane for a couple of hours. I was showing off a little, doing some minor acrobatics, and one of the guys said, "I'm not feeling so good."

"There's a sick bag in the little slot in front of you," I said. But before I had even finished my sentence he basically projectile-vomited all over my back, all over the controls, all over my hands, and all over everything in the plane. Now keep in mind that we were halfway between two cities. There was no place to land, we couldn't even open a window, and there was throw-up all over my shoulder and hands and all over the control panel. It was un-fucking-believable. When we finally landed, the rest of us scrambled out, gagging, and each us proceeded to throw up on the tarmac.

By summer, I'd met another girl and was sort of in love again, and in good weather I would sometimes take her up to Lake Pigeon, about an hour outside of Edmonton. Harry Pinchin, our trumpet player, had a little cabin there, and we'd go swimming and sailing and just kick back. My new girlfriend ended up getting pregnant, and I offered to marry her, but she wasn't interested in marriage. "I just want you to help me through the pregnancy," she said.

When it came time to deliver the baby, I accompanied her to the hospital, and just before we went into the delivery room we had to fill out some paperwork. In the slot that asked for my occupation I wrote—for the first time in my life, and with great pride— *MUSICIAN*. A few hours later, I was the proud father of a little girl, but within two minutes a nurse came into the delivery room and took our baby away. I was heartbroken, but at that point neither of us was really equipped to become parents, and both my girlfriend and the baby disappeared from my life as quickly as they'd come into it.

I went back to work and stayed busy, and tried not to think too deeply about my life, and one night, while I was playing at the club, who should walk in but Ronnie Hawkins. Hawkins is one of the more entertaining characters on the planet. He was in his early thirties at the time, and he was a key player in the Toronto music scene, but he was known by rock aficionados all over the world, and was in fact responsible for launching The Band, Janis Joplin, and David Clayton-Thomas, lead singer of Blood, Sweat & Tears, all of whom had played for him before breaking into the big time. Some of Hawkins's hits included "Forty Days" (*I'm going to give you forty days to get back home*), "Mary Lou" (*She makes a young man groan and an old man pain*) and "Hey Bo Diddley" (*Bo Diddley done had a farm, and on that farm he had some women, women here, women there, women, women, women everywhere*). Ronnie waltzed into the club that night and stayed to watch the show, and after it was over he came backstage and said, "You know, I'd like to have you in my band." This was a pretty big deal. Ronnie was said to have the Midas touch. Anyone who went through the Hawkins School of Hard Knocks, as he called it, generally graduated to bigger and better things. And that's what I wanted. At age twenty, I'd already had my fill of obscurity. This was a huge opportunity and I wasn't going to let it pass me by.

"I'd love to be in your band," I said.

"Great," he said. "You know any good girl singers?"

"Well, I sort of know this girl from Victoria, B. J. Cook, who might be able to help us. I don't know her well, but she's in Vancouver now, and she knows all the great singers. She's with a band called Sweet Beaver."

Ronnie's eyes lit up. "Well, I sure do like the name of that band," he said. "See if you can track her down. I'd like to hear her."

The next day I went back to my apartment and made a few calls, and I reached B.J. and told her I was looking for a girl singer, for

Ronnie's band. "I know you know everyone," I said. "Can you help us out?"

"What about me?" she said.

"You? Come on! You're not going to leave Sweet Beaver for Ronnie Hawkins." And that's what I thought, honestly. Sweet Beaver was a very hot band.

"No," she said. "I'm serious. I'm looking for a change."

"Well you've got to come fast," I said. "Ronnie's doing a few gigs in Edmonton, but he's going back to Toronto in a week."

Two days later, B.J. came out and auditioned for Ronnie and got hired, and a few days after that I packed up all of my earthly possessions and went to downtown Edmonton and climbed onto Ronnie's big Greyhound bus for the 1,700-mile drive to Toronto. Ronnie was already on board, holding court, and he was drunker than a skunk, and when he saw me he smiled a big smile and said, "It's a good thing you're here. You're driving the bus."

"I am?" I said. "I've never driven a bus in my life."

"There's nothing to it," he said. "Just make wider turns."

After another drink or two, Ronnie got off the bus and climbed into his private camper, with his own personal driver, and off we went. And of course I immediately got lost trying to find the freeway, and I ended up in a ditch on some country road. I had to pay a tow truck to pull us out, but a few hours later we were on our way, and I discovered that there's really not that much to driving a bus. All you need to remember is that everything is bigger, that it takes a long time to slow down, and that—as Ronnie pointed out—you've got to make wider turns. Once you've got that down, you're on your way.

When we got to Toronto, Hawkins put us up in his offices, so we were all living on mattresses on the floor in rooms with only one tiny window. He had promised us luxurious suites in the heart of downtown Toronto, and this place was a dump with no heat. It was so cold, in fact, that one morning I looked through the small window and saw a cat out there, with one little paw in the air, like he was going somewhere. Only he was dead, frozen stiff—that's how cold it was. A little cat frozen dead right outside the window.

I still remember our very first rehearsal together because Ronnie showed up buck-naked. "Boys," he said, "let's everybody take off our clothes. We might get lucky one day and get a chance to play in a nudist colony, and it's always good to be prepared."

A few nights later he took us to a party where he staged a Big Dick Contest. "Don't show them that whole thing," he said. "Just take out enough to win."

Ronnie tried to be generous with us so that we could begin looking around for decent places to live. "Whatever I get, the rest of the band gets half," he said, and he was true to his word. He was making $2,500 a week, so the rest of us—B.J., me, and four other guys—ended up sharing $1,250. And just in case any of us doubted him, he made a point of showing us the contracts. "See? There it is in black and white: Twenty-five hundred bucks. I don't want any bad blood between us."

I thought that was a smart thing to do, and the lesson has stayed with me to this day: It pays to be up front with the people you work with.

Unfortunately, it wasn't enough money to move into a place of our own—B.J. and I had become a couple by then—so we continued to live in that drafty little icebox. One night, lying on the lumpy mattress next to B.J., I heard a knock at the door. I stumbled out of bed in the dark and opened it a crack and saw Ronnie standing in the shadows. "Wake up, boy," he said. "I want to introduce you to someone." He had a big grin on his face, and I looked down and saw that his pants were down around his ankles, and that a woman was on her knees in front of him. "I want you to meet Miss Toronto," he said.

"Nice to meet you," I said, but she was busy and couldn't answer, and she sort of half-smiled up at me and I returned the smile and shut the door and crawled back into bed.

B.J. stirred under the covers beside me. "What's going on?" she said sleepily.

"Nothing," I said. "Just a bad dream."

Within a few weeks, B.J. and I finally had enough money to rent a small apartment, and we settled in together. She was seven years older than me, and she had a nine-year-old daughter, Tamre, who lived mostly with B.J.'s parents, back in Victoria, and who would come to visit us from time to time. I was twenty years old and didn't know anything about being a father, so I treated her like a little sister.

Musically, I wasn't feeling particularly challenged, but I liked the whole Ronnie Hawkins experience, especially hanging out after the show and listening to the man talk. He was a bit of a philosopher, and this is where I first heard that great bit of advice: "Boy, most people, when they come up against a brick wall, they just keep hitting their heads against it until they knock themselves out. Hell, half of them don't even *know* they're hitting a wall. But if you open your eyes, and you try to recognize what's going on, you'll learn to retreat and attack from another direction." I liked the sound of what he was telling me, but it would be years before I really understood it.

My mother used to say something similar, but she put it into her own words. "When one door closes, another one opens." She also used to say, "It's not what you know, but who you know," and in retrospect that really surprises me. She was talking about networking before that word had become part of our general vocabulary, and I don't know when or how she came up with that idea.

One night, Chuck Berry was in Toronto, and I took B.J. to see him. (I finally understood that his contribution to the world of music was nothing short of monumental.) After the show, I went backstage to say hello, thinking maybe I'd impress B.J. a little, but the guy didn't even remember me. Then again, why would he? The bastard hadn't even spoken to me when I was playing backup for him in London.

We stayed with Ronnie Hawkins for about six months, and toured eastern Canada with him, and I became the official Greyhound bus driver, but one evening, shortly after we got back to Toronto, Ronnie took me aside for a little talk. "Son," he said, "you are one of the best musicians around. You play like Bach and Mozart. But you're a cadaver on stage. I need people that move around."

"I move around," I protested.

"No you don't," he said. "And I'll tell you the truth: I'd rather go with the guy that doesn't play quite as good but at least looks like he's havin' fun."

"I'm having fun," I said.

"No you're not," he said. "You look like you've just been to your mother's funeral. Plus I don't think you really like playing my music."

He was right about that. I wasn't crazy about his music. I'd been playing it for six months and it hadn't even begun to grow on me.

A moment later, B.J. walked into the office. "What's going on?" she said.

"Ronnie just fired me," I said. "He says I play like a cadaver."

"He did? You do?"

Ronnie turned to look at her. "Now listen, I know you two are together, but I like you, B.J., so I'm going to give you a choice. You can stay with the band, which would be my first choice, because I think you're a really good singer, or you can go with the cadaver."

And B.J. said, "I'll go with the cadaver."

A week later, B.J. and I were living in Vancouver. We were lying in bed one afternoon, with the rain beating against the windows, and she turned to look at me and said, "What would you like to do?"

"What do you mean?" I asked.

"Like if you could put the perfect band together, who would be in it?"

I started naming local musicians—some of the guys I'd grown up with, and some talented strangers. There was Doug Edwards, a guitar player who'd been on the road with the Fifth Dimension—that was a huge deal to me. And I liked Duris Maxwell, an amazing drummer who was wildly unpredictable, on and off the drums. (His original name was Ted Lewis, and I have no idea when he came up with Duris Maxwell, or why.) Then there was Donny Gerrard, a black guy, a truly amazing local singer, and two other guys—Steve Pugsley and Carl Graves.

The next thing I knew, B.J. was making calls, and before long we had a band. We got pretty much everybody we wanted, and we went out and began rehearsing. When we felt like we'd rehearsed enough, we went to see Ralph Harding, who ran a place in Vancouver called Studio 3, and made a demo. We called ourselves Skylark.

One day, this guy Barry DeVorzon showed up in Vancouver, from Los Angeles, and went to visit his friend Ralph. Barry fell in love with "Wildflower," one of the songs, and with our band. "Goddamn it!" he told us. "That is a hit song! I'm in the music business and I'm going to bring you guys to L.A."

I didn't know it then, but Barry was about to become a pivotal person in my life. And he wasn't kidding about being in the music business. A lot of guys are just talk, but Barry had written a song called "Nadia's Theme," with Perry Botkin, Jr., for daytime television's *The Young and the Restless,* and he'd also had the good sense to sign The Association, so he had heat. He went back to L.A. with a copy of our demo and did his best to sell it, and after a couple of weeks, while he was still making the rounds, he invited B.J. and me to fly down to visit. He picked us up at the airport in a beautiful brand-new Jaguar, and he drove us to Sunset Boulevard and pulled up to the curb and pointed at a huge billboard. It was for a movie called *Bless the Beasts & Children,* and down near the bottom, in massive letters, it said "MUSIC BY BARRY DEVORZON." I thought, *My God! This is huge!*

On our way to the hotel, I realized that I *needed* to be in L.A. The city just felt right to me. This is where it all happened. This is where every single musician whose name I had ever seen on an album cover had come to make his or her mark. This is where I *belonged*. Ever since that I've often wondered if other people are like that—that they arrive in a new city and it hits them, *Here I am, where I belong.*

That night, Barry took us to Benihana for dinner. And some Japanese guy cooked right at our table! This was the most amazing thing I had ever seen. This was the big time for sure! L.A. was definitely the shit!

For the next few days, Barry ran around town trying to push our tape. He kept telling people, "Goddamn it, this 'Wildflower' song is a hit," but nobody was biting. He got us a meeting with Russ Regan, over at MCA Records—he arranged a lunch, actually, which I didn't realize was a big deal—and Russ liked the song and the group, so we were off to a good start. Then I asked him how he was going to promote the album, and Russ fidgeted a little and said, "We'll put some thought into that." I glanced over at Barry. He was looking at me like he wanted to kill me, but that didn't stop me.

"What about an advance?" I said.

I believe Barry kicked me under the table at that point, but I ignored him. Maybe I was just a naïve kid from Canada, but I knew what I needed, and I was waiting for Russ's answer. "I'm not giving you an advance," he said finally. "I'm giving you a record deal, and that's enough—it's *more* than enough."

"Not to me," I said. "I'm not signing with you. There are seven of us. We need to eat. We need to go back home and get our stuff and drive down here. We need to survive."

Russ Regan must have thought I was crazy, and I know Barry sure did. "They've got Elton John on their label," Barry said later. "They've got Neil Diamond. What is wrong with you? How can you blow this deal?"

"We won't survive without an advance," I said.

Barry tried to save the deal, and he got on the phone to Russ later that same afternoon, but Russ wanted no part of me. "I'm going to pass on this one," he said. "I think that young man could be trouble."

Then B.J. got in touch with this guy Dino Airali, who ran Shelter Records. She'd met him years earlier, in L.A., and he came over to the hotel to see us. He listened to the demo and was clearly impressed. "This is great," he said. "I'm going to go over to Capitol Records to see if I can get you a deal." And that's exactly what he did. He went over to Capitol Records and got us a record deal, and he had one of his lawyer friends, Abe Somers, negotiate the terms. So really, when you think about it, at the end of the day it all happened thanks to B.J.'s connections, and we scored a $20,000 advance—which in those days was a huge amount of money.

I immediately went out and bought a Volkswagen van, since the band was going to need transportation, and then I told everyone that they'd be getting $50 a week—this was 1971, and in those days you could actually manage on that—and a few days later we rented a big house with a pool in a nice neighborhood near the airport. Then we went back to Vancouver, packed everything into the van, and made the long return drive to Los Angeles. We drove straight through. We made the occasional pit stop, switching drivers whenever we got tired, and arrived in Los Angeles in almost exactly twenty-four hours.

As soon as we got into town, exhausted and hungry, we parked across the street from the old Carlton Lodge, on Highland Avenue, where we were going to be staying until the house was ready, and before we checked in we hit the restaurant and grabbed some lunch. When we finished lunch, we returned to the van and found it empty.

Someone had come along in broad daylight and taken everything we owned: the instruments, my albums, seven suitcases, a sewing machine, the keyboard my parents had bought me—all of it. I couldn't believe it. I was in love with this city, and within an hour of our arrival we'd been ripped off. We checked into the hotel and I went up to the room and sat on the bed and cried, and an hour later we walked to the nearest precinct and filed a police report. On our way out, I looked at B.J. and she looked at me, and I decided I was in love with L.A. again. "Well," I said. "We're here to make a record. Let's go make a record."

"Wildflower," our debut single, was written by our guitarist, Doug Edwards, and a cop buddy of mine from Canada, Dave Richardson. Dave used to hang out and watch us jam when we were playing in Victoria, and my mother was convinced he was an undercover cop. "The only reason he's there is to bust you for drugs," she used to tell me. "If not you, some of your musician friends." I thought that was kind of funny. I had told her countless times that I didn't do drugs, and that Dave was a great friend who loved music as much as I did, but she couldn't help being a mother—she was always looking out for me.

To this day I am amazed by the lyrics Dave wrote for that song. *Let her cry, for she's a lady / Let her dream, for she's a child / Let the rain fall down upon her / She's a free and gentle flower, growing wild.* He was a deep, compassionate guy with a heart of gold, and maybe he would have become a hugely successful lyricist, but after twenty-five years as a detective he became a missionary priest and ended up in Israel, taking care of homeless kids.

"Wildflower" reached the Top 10 on the *Billboard* charts. I was blown away. I began to think, as I had told my father, mistakenly, that the music business was nowhere near as tough as people said it was.

But there were a few things that helped make "Wildflower" a success. There was Al Corey, for starters, a promoter at Capitol Records who was absolutely relentless about pushing the song; and there was a radio station in Windsor, Ontario, that played the record over and over again, to fulfill its commitment to "Canadian content." (Luckily for us, the station had such a powerful signal that on a clear night you could hear it all the way to Miami.) The song itself was good, of course, which certainly helped sell it, and our singer, Donny Gerrard, was astonishingly good, and those amazing vocals of his really put us over the top.

Donny was an interesting guy. Everybody liked him, but it was really hard to make music with him because he was the most noncommittal person I have ever met. You could ask him ten different ways if he liked something, and you'd never get much of an answer. "Yeah, it's okay." "It's not bad." "I'm not sure." He didn't really seem to like anything, and as it turned out he didn't even like our stuff. One day we were driving along in the van, and "Wildflower" came on the radio, and he reached over and turned to another station.

"What are you doing?" I said. "That's our hit record!"

"You know," he said, "I don't really care for that kind of music."

I was floored. I could never get this guy to tell me what he liked. He never once said a single word—positive or negative—about anything, not my work and not anybody else's, and it made me crazy—because I couldn't understand how a guy with a voice like that could be so devoid of passion.

"What the hell *do* you like, Donny?" I asked him again, somewhat more forcefully than usual.

He took a moment to think about it, then said: "I like Earth, Wind & Fire."

"Funny you should say that," I said. "I love Earth, Wind & Fire." It was true. Whenever they released a new album, I was one of those guys who'd be standing in line at midnight at Tower Records, waiting to be among the first to buy it.

With "Wildflower" still riding the charts, and the album selling respectably, Capitol Records really got behind us. We toured with Loggins & Messina and Ten Years After, and we made an appearance on *The Midnight Special,* a weekly television show that focused on hot bands.

Kenny Loggins was a lot more communicative than the guys we

played with in London, and he made us feel like we were part of the show. I remember hanging out with him in the dressing room one night, just before we went on stage, and he began playing a song he'd been working on: *And even though we ain't got money / I'm so in love with you honey / And everything will bring a chain of love.*

That was "Danny's Song," of course, and it went on to become a huge hit for him.

After that gig ended, we found a manager, Ric Bowen, and he moved us to Fort Lauderdale for a while, where it was easier to book jobs. B.J. and I ended up getting married at his place, in his backyard. A justice of the peace did the honors, and the only guests were the manager and the guys in the band.

The next day B.J. and I went to the Bahamas, for a three-day honeymoon, but we were broke and we were a little shocked by the prices. A dollar for a milkshake? I don't think so! The hotel was nothing to write home about, either. The first night, we came across the biggest cockroach either of us had ever seen—it must have been four inches across. We didn't want to kill it, though, so we put the metal trash bin over it, and for the rest of the night we could hear it throwing its little carapace against the bin, trying desperately to escape.

Then our second album came out and tanked—we didn't know what we were doing, and it wasn't a good album—and Skylark broke up.

I was in shock. This was exactly what had happened to me in London: Things got a little rough and everybody split. I couldn't understand how anyone could even *think* like that. We'd had one good album. The second one tanked. So what? It happens. The point was to keep trying. But the guys had had enough. They were giving up and going home. "You're crazy," I said. "This is no time to quit. I'm going back to Los Angeles." They didn't listen. They flew from Miami to Vancouver, and B.J. and I returned to L.A.

I don't know honestly what gave me the strength or the confidence to keep fighting. Maybe I knew, instinctively, despite our early success with "Wildflower," that it wasn't going to be easy. Maybe it was that same thing that took me to a person's door at age twelve, announcing, "I'm David Foster. From the Starbright Combo. I'm here about the financial arrangements." And of course the other element was that I knew I belonged in Los Angeles. I'd been all over—London, Toronto, Edmonton, Vancouver—but only Los Angeles felt right from the very start. I wasn't leaving. It was as simple as that. I was *home*.

A few weeks after B.J. and I returned to Los Angeles, while we were trying to figure out what we were going to do make a living, I heard that Bill Evans—one of the jazz greats, my idol, my hero—was going to be playing at Shelly's Manne-Hole, a local club. I was so excited that we got there at six, three hours before the show, and we sat there sipping Cokes and waiting for Bill Evans to show up. When the show finally got underway, it was beyond anything I had imagined, and after the first set I actually managed to get close to him and fawn a little. I told him about my friend Rick Reynolds, who had gone out of his way to teach me what jazz was all about, and I said that Evans was a big favorite of his, too.

During the second set, I took my eyes off the stage for a moment and noticed that there were only about twenty people in the room. That was a real shock to me. Evans was one of the greatest piano players on the planet, a living legend, and he was playing to a near-empty room. That was a rude awakening. I loved jazz, and in the back of my mind I always thought I'd get back to it at some point, but I needed to make a living, and it didn't look as if jazz was any way to do that.

Then B.J. got pregnant—this was late in '72. We had bills to pay and no prospects and pretty soon there'd be another mouth to feed. Desperate, I went out and knocked on doors, and I ended up getting work as a piano player for a company that auditioned actors for theatrical productions—things like *Godspell* and *Grease* and *Jesus Christ, Superstar*. And that's what I did all day: I played piano at cattle calls for

63

five bucks an hour. Some people would think that was beneath them—especially for a guy who'd recently come off a hit record, toured with Loggins & Messina, and appeared on *The Midnight Special*—but to me it really didn't feel that way. My mother's words stayed with me—"When one door closes, another one opens"—and I honestly believed them to be true. I knew I would meet new people through the job, and that, statistically speaking, some of them had to be the right people.

At first, of course, I met a lot of the *wrong* people. I'd be out there on stage, and a guy would come out looking like he was high on something, and he's snap his fingers at me and say, "Give me a little Van Morrison."

I'd want to say, "Any particular song, asshole?" But of course I couldn't say that. So I'd take a wild guess and try my luck with "Brown Eyed Girl" or "Moondance" or something until I made him happy.

Whenever a singer sounded bad, he or she would scowl at me and look out at the producer, sitting in the shadows near the front, and he or she always said the same thing: "He didn't play it properly." I'm sure some of them were right. I didn't know anything about Broadway shows, I had never seen a Broadway play in my life, and from the little I'd heard I wasn't impressed by Broadway musicals. So, yeah, I'm sure half the time I *did* play it wrong. It didn't bother me, though. I just kept playing. I was making five bucks an hour, and, being frugal by nature, I knew I could save half of that.

Then one day I got a call about auditioning for Loggins & Messina, and I was very excited. I had really liked those guys. They were up in Ojai, about an hour north of Los Angeles, and I drove up with Willy Ornealus, a drummer friend of mine who happened to have a car. When we got there, their drummer wasn't around, so I told them that my friend was a drummer, and they invited him to play along. He ended up getting the gig; I didn't. I was crushed. We didn't talk much on the drive back to L.A.

In July 1973, B.J. gave birth to our daughter, Amy Skylark. By this time we were living in our own home, a modest little house on Blix Street, in North Hollywood, and I was genuinely excited at the prospect of fatherhood, but I didn't know much about babies and I wasn't particularly helpful. B.J. was an expert, of course—or should have been anyway, since this was her second child—so I let her take care of things at home and I continued to let myself be abused by second-rate, wannabe singers.

Before long, as expected, I started meeting some interesting people. One day I found myself sitting in front of a piano in a small ballet studio with Gene Kelly. No agents, no manager, no handlers. We were waiting for the gorgeous Cheryl Ladd, who had come in to audition for him, and she was in back getting dressed or something.

It was taking such a long time that I just couldn't help myself. "Mr. Kelly," I said. "Any chance you could show me how you did that thing where you danced on a newspaper?" I don't know how many people remember the movie *Summer Stock,* with Judy Garland, but that's where the sketch is from—and it's a classic. Gene Kelly walks across a creaky wooden floor and starts tap dancing. And there's an open sheet of newspaper on the floor. And when he taps the paper, it makes a different, slightly muted sound. Before long he's whistling and tapping and dancing, and he ends up cutting the newspaper in half, with his feet, and then cutting one of those halves into perfect quarters.

"Why, sure!" Mr. Kelly said. And he got up and did it for me. And as he did, he explained that when they first filmed the sequence the newspaper kept sliding out from under him. "We had to keep getting new pieces of paper, and we had to make sure they all looked the same, with the same headline and everything, and it wasn't nearly as smooth as it looked on film."

Then Cheryl Ladd came out and I did what I was being paid to do, play piano, and I think it went well because she ended up inviting me to a party—my first Hollywood party. Cheryl was married to David

Ladd, son of the legendary actor Alan Ladd, and when B.J. and I walked into the house we saw Donna Reed, the first real Hollywood celebrity I'd ever seen. B.J. pointed her out in an almost reverential whisper, and I don't believe I'd ever seen her looking so impressed. She was a big fan of *The Donna Reed Show,* along with all those old black-and-white movies, so this was very exciting for her. She kept pointing to people I didn't recognize: Red Buttons, Jack Albertson from *Chico and the Man,* some guy from *77 Sunset Strip.* It went on and on, but I wasn't impressed.

I was impressed only once, in fact, and that was the day O. J. Simpson was there. O.J. and Cheryl had done a movie together a couple of years earlier, *Jamaica Reef,* and they were still friends, and shortly after I arrived at the party I actually went out of my way to shake O.J.'s hand.

Cheryl also had us over for tea once, just the family. My mother had come to visit from Victoria, to spend a little time with her grand-daughter, and Cheryl invited us over and gave us a tour of the house. She took us into this one special room that was filled with all sorts of things that had belonged to David's father, who had starred in *Shane* and countless other movies. She showed us his silver hairbrush, his nail clippers, his golf shoes, and a bunch of other memorabilia—and for B.J. it was almost a religious experience. But my mother and I weren't that impressed, and in fact I'm not sure my mother even knew who Alan Ladd was. I think she thought he was Allen Ludden, the host of *Password,* a television game show.

We kept getting invited back to Cheryl's parties, and I often found myself at the piano, providing some of the entertainment. I didn't mind, though, because we had fun, and we made friends. One of those new friends was Liz Torres, a comedian, and one day she asked me to accompany her to an audition for the theatrical version of *The Rocky Horror Picture Show.* We got up on stage and did our thing, and as soon as she stopped singing the producer said, "Well, she's not right for this, but we're interested in you. How would you like to be our piano player? We're opening at the Roxy in two weeks."

That was just like what had happened with Loggins & Messina, but in reverse. I felt a little bad for Liz, but she was talented—I knew she'd get something.

And that's how I became the piano player on *The Rocky Horror Picture Show*, with Tim Curry and Meat Loaf and a cast of crazies. It was my first regular job in L.A.—my first regular, weekly paycheck as an adult. I was making three hundred dollars a week, which was fantastic, and every night everyone would show up about half an hour before the show and jam for about twenty minutes. By the end of the first week, I was pretty much running those little jam sessions, and by the end of the second week I think I became, unofficially, the music director. I was just doing what I loved doing, and my energy seemed to fuel the rest of the guys in the band, so it worked out nicely.

And every night would bring fresh surprises in the audience. I'd see Liz Taylor in the front row, say, or Diana Ross, or Clint Eastwood. The show was a huge hit. Everyone in Hollywood came to watch it. But for me the real excitement was being up on stage, playing with professional musicians. They weren't the top-tier guys, admittedly, but most of them were pretty accomplished, and some of them had done a little studio work. I had known this would lead to something, and I was right. One night I met Jim Keltner, a drummer—I think he was subbing for the regular drummer—and he introduced me to William "Smitty" Smith, a brilliant organist who ran weekly jam sessions at the original Record Plant, the recording studio on Third Street that later burned down. They invited me to come down the following Sunday and I was very excited. The place was famous. All the name musicians hung out at the Record Plant. This was the big time.

B.J. was very encouraging, as always, despite the fact that our marriage had entered a rocky phase. That Sunday, as usual, I left her back at the house, with Amy, and went off to see Smitty and Jim at the Record Plant. They introduced me to some of the other players, and Smitty parked me in front of the piano, which was off to one side, facing the wall. Whenever you're playing, whether you're recording or just jamming, you don't want the sound of the drums leaking into the piano, so you always look for good separation, and you do this by isolating the piano.

So I sat with my back to the other players, and I put on my headphones, and we started jamming. And as time passed, the music would get lighter and lighter. Suddenly there would be no bass. And then the guitars would fade out. And then there wouldn't be any drums. And before long I'd be sitting there playing by myself, but I just kept going.

Eventually I figured out that, one by one, the guys were going into the back rooms to do drugs. And it was a really weird place. The rooms had different names, like "French Whore Room," or "Rack Room," or "Torture Room," and all the rooms had beds in them. But I didn't go back there. I kept playing. I was just happy to be there. And eventually the bass would come back in, followed by the drums and the guitars, and then I'd hear the sax, and we were jamming again. And I absolutely loved it. I went back every Sunday night, and Jim Keltner introduced me to everyone. John Lennon. Van Morrison. Joe Cocker. Mick Jagger.

I usually wouldn't get home till morning, and I felt bad about it, but not bad enough to stop doing it. I honestly didn't know how to be a proper husband. B.J. was a talented singer in her own right, but she had given up her career to take care of our child and to try to make a home for us. It wasn't fair, and I don't imagine it ever is. I owed her a lot. She had been instrumental in putting Skylark together, and it was her connections that eventually got us that first deal with Capitol Records, and now she was stuck at home while I was exploding as a studio musician.

This probably sounds old-fashioned to many people, and I'm sure it was—but that's how we did things back then. The husband went out and earned the money, the wife stayed home, and the marriage slowly unraveled. And when *Rocky Horror* closed, with things at home getting progressively worse, I began spending more and more time at the Record Plant, and started making connections there that led to session work.

I became pretty well known as a session player, one of the top three or four piano players in the business, and people would call and book me for different gigs. Keltner was instrumental in making this happen for me, and I kept running into other people who appreciated my talent and my work ethic, and they kept me busy, constantly pushing me onto bigger and better things. I remember getting a call from Frank DeCaro, a well-known music contractor, who asked me if I was available to play with Mac Davis, then a hugely successful country singer. We booked it for the following Monday, and the weekend before the gig I decided I wanted to get a tan and I went outside and fell asleep on my stomach. Luckily I was wearing a shirt, but the backs of my legs got so badly fried that I ended up at the burn unit of the local hospital.

I showed up for my first session with Mac Davis on crutches, and during a break I overheard DeCaro talking to someone on the phone about me. "I got this new kid who's really good, but he's a gimp," he said. "I think he's got polio or something."

I then booked a gig with Helen Reddy, which was equally exciting, and I met her husband and manager, Jeff Wald. He had a reputation as a very tough manager, and I heard a famous story that he once walked into Capitol Records and pissed on the desk of a promoter who had failed to get enough radio stations to play one of his client's records. I remember thinking, *Now there's a guy who really fights for his artists.*

I got so busy that I bought a little date book to keep track of everything, and my days were very, very full. Usually, I would do commercial jingles in the morning, from eight to ten, say. Or background music for such shows as *Wheel of Fortune, Facts of Life,* and *Diff'rent Strokes* with my friend Alan Thicke, a fellow Canadian. (I loved it. I was doing music. I didn't care what it was.) Then I would do sessions from ten to one, from two to five, and from seven to midnight.

In the early part of the day, I would be playing for Glen Campbell or Neil Sedaka—the MOR (middle of the road) stuff. And at night I'd find myself playing with Ringo Starr or Dolly Parton—just about anyone who was recording and needed a good piano player. I worked with Toto and the Fifth Dimension and Small Faces. I kept meeting people and was having a blast. Plus it made for interesting opportunities. If the producer was weak, for example, I might help him come up with the intros, and I'd make other suggestions as we went along, and from time to time it seemed as if I was taking over the guy's job. But if the producer was strong, and if he had a good arranger, I'd just do what I was being paid to do—be a robot and play. I loved every minute of it, though. I couldn't believe I was being paid to do music, and I was happy doing any kind of music.

As night fell, I'd go home and sleep for four or five hours, and in the morning the whole cycle would start again, with the jingles, and I was making just north of $100,000 a year. Back in the early seventies, that was a huge amount of money.

From time to time the person who was calling to book the session would ask about my drug of choice. I guess they wanted to keep their session players happy. "I like chocolate chip cookies and milk," I'd say, and they invariably thought this was some kind of code—that I didn't want to share anything over the phone. So I'd have to set them straight: "No, that's what I really like. If you have chocolate chip cookies and milk for me, I will be very happy."

I also worked on some big hits during this period, including *The Dream Weaver,* Gary Wright's album—thanks again to Jim Keltner, who played drums on that. Wright had actually done an earlier album with Spooky Tooth, another band, but I believe this was his first solo outing. Now that I think about it, it was also the first time I was asked to work on an entire album, on every single track. Gary was a great musician, and he taught me a lot about synthesizers. He was the very first person to show me a string synthesizer. One afternoon he called me over. "Come here," he said. "I want you to see something." I looked at what I thought was a regular keyboard and, at his urging, reached out and touched it. A string sound came out and I almost shit myself. I couldn't believe you could get a violin sound out of a keyboard!

Gary gave me credit on the album as a keyboard player, which meant a lot to me. The fact that *The Dream Weaver* went on to sell upward of ten million copies only made it that much sweeter.

The action never stopped. I played with Booker T. and the M.G.'s, and with Kenny Rogers, and I played on a string of Rod Stewart albums. Stewart would always roll into the studio with a beautiful blonde on his arm, a wife or a girlfriend—I could never tell which—and he'd always pause about a minute into the session. "Let's go one key higher," he'd suggest. And we would. A minute later, same thing: "Let's go one key higher." He'd keep doing this until he was belting out the songs at the top of his range, which I think was one of the keys to his success.

I also played, briefly, with Neil Diamond. Or with his *band,* anyway. Sometimes you'll show up at the rehearsal studio and you'll play with the musicians, for days and weeks on end, and the main guy shows up only when you're done rehearsing—when you're ready for him. I never even saw Neil, and, in his perpetual absence, Alan Lindgren, a talented keyboard player and arranger, was running the show. I think he was a little threatened by my talent, so one night—after I think I'd performed admirably well—he asked me not to come back.

To this day I enjoy telling people that I was fired by Neil Diamond.

Another guy I worked with was Paul Anka, a fellow Canadian. I met him at the studio. I'd been called in to play on one of his records, and we instantly became good friends. But I must admit that I broke one of the Ten Commandments with Paul. I *coveted* him. He had the life I wanted. At one point he invited me to come work with him in Carmel, where he lived with his wife and five daughters in a spectacular hilltop home with endless ocean views. He had a recording studio in the house, and he taught me a lot about songwriting. He also taught me about wine, and about which fork to use at a state dinner, in case that ever happened, and about the joys of private air travel.

One time, Paul told me, "I'm going to buy you for two million dollars." It sounded like a good deal, and I think he meant it, but I passed. (In retrospect, it would have been a very good deal—for *him*.)

A few years later I was having trouble getting my green card and Paul put a call in to a high-level government official—I'm talking about a guy who spent a lot of time in the Oval Office—and the problem was immediately taken care of. For some crazy reason, I had to go to San Francisco to pick up the card, and Paul took care of that, too— he flew up with me in his private jet. It was a Lear, and to this day I'm addicted to private jet travel, arguably the greatest perk on the planet.

I also happen to remember the conversation I had with Paul on the short flight to San Francisco. "I came from nothing, and when I started touring I used to ride on buses everywhere," he said. "For years and years I was in those lousy buses, so my dream was to get a plane of my own. The kids in music today, they are so spoiled. They have no idea what it was like back then."

The session work continued, and one afternoon the phone rang and a familiar voice said, "Hullo, David, this is old Harrison here. I was chatting with Jim Keltner, and he says you play all right."

It was *George* Harrison.

I was struck mute for a moment, but I quickly found my voice. "Keltner says I play all right, does he?"

"Won't you come down?" he said. He was very casual about it, but I was a nervous wreck. I kept thinking, *I'm talking to George Harrison. He was one of the Beatles. This can't be happening. I'm just a kid from Victoria.*

I went down to the studio and met Harrison, and he was mellow and very friendly, as if he were just a normal guy, not a demigod. He wasn't very talkative, however, so I didn't get any great stories out of him, but I know he liked my work, because a few weeks later he flew me to London to help with the arrangements on two albums, *Extra Texture* and *33 1/3*, which were released in 1975 and 1976, respectively. I wrote several string arrangements for both of them, and I worked hard, but neither album was the hit we'd hoped for.

Maybe I was part of the reason; I don't know.

When I got back to L.A., I kept doing session work, and it was beginning to wear me down. The money was nice, and I was moving up the ladder—from demo pay, to scale, to double scale, to triple scale, etc.—but I could see some of the older guys moving in the opposite direction, *down* the ladder. They'd been doing it too long, and some of them had clearly lost their enthusiasm for the work, and it showed. And of course as a result they were no longer valued as musicians, and the younger guys started taking their jobs. I was one of those younger guys, and I realized that I didn't want to turn into one of the unhappy older guys, so I started thinking about other options.

The first thing that occurred to me was that I had the talent to become a producer. I had worked for dozens of producers, and at times I had even found myself doing the jobs of some of the weaker ones, and I realized that most of them didn't know very much about music. I would watch those producers flailing around and it was clear to me that they survived by getting the studio musicians, guys like me, to do their jobs for them. It kind of pissed me off, to be honest. Many of these guys were complete bullshitters. They didn't know an A from a

B, or a G from an A, and when they started talking in colors—"It should be more pink, and the intro should be more blue"—you knew you were in serious trouble.

Then one day I was called to a big studio session at the Record Plant, and I found out that I was going to be working with Barbra Streisand, who was already an icon. I held her in the highest regard, so I was really looking forward to it. We all were. Some thirty orchestra members, three guitar players, and two drummers. I was one of several keyboard players. The producer was Rupert Holmes, a really sweet guy who had a number-one pop hit with "Escape," better known as "The Piña Colada Song," and he waited with the rest of us.

Suddenly, I *felt* her presence, and I looked up and saw that she had just walked into the room. She was so far away as to be almost indistinguishable, but to this day I credit her—and that moment—for helping me formulate my definition of a superstar: It's a person whose presence you feel in a room even if you don't see them, and whose absence is palpable as soon as they leave. And I will tell you this: Barbra had that in spades.

She and Rupert talked for a bit, and then we got to work. We were doing a Stevie Wonder song, "All in Love Is Fair," and the arrangement felt a little bombastic. I didn't like it, and Barbra certainly didn't like it, and she and Rupert went back and forth on how to change it, and I tried to listen to what she was telling him. Finally, we plunged in for the eighth or ninth time. The music started up, Barbra began to sing, and I was off in my isolated corner, playing my piano. A few bars into it, Barbra stopped, *again*. She looked very frustrated. "No, no, no," she said. "It's just not right. That's not the way it needs to be." And at that point we broke for lunch.

Now I'm not sure the average person understands this, but if you're in a room with three or four musicians, trying to make a record, and something doesn't sound right, it's easy to make changes on the spot.

You stop and try something else. You'll say, "I think the drum should come in eight bars later." Or, "I don't like that guitar lick. Try it down an octave." Whatever. In a matter of minutes, you get your point across and you're rocking again. But when you're dealing with an orchestra, you can't do that, because writing orchestra parts takes hours, if not days or weeks. Clearly, I was aware of the scope of the problem, and—ever the opportunist—I didn't go to lunch. I stayed behind, noodling at the piano, playing the song the way I thought it should be played, and the way I thought Barbra wanted it to be played, based on what I'd been able to pick up from her conversations with Rupert.

And suddenly I heard that familiar voice: "Hey you! What is that?"

It was Barbra. She walked over and I felt like a character in a movie.

As she floated toward me, I thought she looked truly magnificent. She seemed to be glowing, actually, and she had diamonds-by-the-yard around both wrists, simple silver chains with modest diamonds at six-inch intervals. When I noticed her hands, I thought they were absolutely the most beautiful hands I had ever seen. In short, I was completely star-struck. She was absolutely stunning.

"What was that you just played?" she asked. "Can you play it again?"

"It was just, well—I thought the whole thing could be simpler," I said. I know my voice was shaking, so I looked down at the keys and played a little lick. "You could open with just the vocal and the piano," I suggested, "and bring the bass in, and have the orchestra follow a little later." I played a little more. I was too intimidated to look at her directly.

"Yeah, I like that!" she said. She turned around. "Rupert! Did you hear that? Let's do it like that!" She turned to look at me again and smiled, and her whole face lit up. "That was great," she said. "That's the way we're going to do it."

Rupert came out and she made me play it for him the way I'd just played it for her, and when the rest of the session players came back from lunch we did it my way. After an orchestral intro, the first half of that song was just Barbra and me—Barbra on vocals, me on the piano. And the orchestra came in on the second half. I felt like a producer.

I had saved the day. Barbra was happy, Rupert was relieved, and every last one of us came out a winner. I remember hoping that she'd remember me, and that perhaps I'd laid the groundwork for future collaborations.

Two weeks later, still slogging away in the session trenches, and still weighing my options, Jim Keltner called to ask me if I'd be interested in being part of a band.

"You don't have to ask," I said.

Jim introduced me to Danny Kortchmar, a great and unique guitar player, and Paul Stallworth, a bassist, and we called ourselves Attitudes. We did two albums for Dark Horse, George Harrison's label, and if I remember correctly we recorded mostly at A&M Records. Harrison was such a low-key guy that he was okay with anything and everything we did.

Unfortunately, neither of the albums created so much as a ripple. And it's funny, because thirty years later I ran into Harrison's widow, Olivia, and she couldn't stop talking about those recordings. "We should get those tapes," she said. "That band was so good. We should dig them up and put them out there again. It was really great stuff."

I think I have to agree with her. Some of the tracks were really pretty good, but we never did anything to promote them. We were just a group of studio guys trying to make good music together, but we were a little spoiled, too: We were making too much money as session musicians to take time off to promote the work.

• • •

There's one more George Harrison story I'd like to share . . .

One night, not long after Attitudes had faded into early obscurity, Keltner and I and a couple of other guys were over at Harrison's house, on Carolwood, having a drink or two and listening to music. Ringo Starr was there, too, and suddenly I had an idea. "Hey," I said. "Why don't we call John and Paul and tell them to come over?"

I knew both of them were in town, and for some crazy reason I had convinced myself they just might do it.

Harrison looked across at me and said, "Yeah. That's not a bad idea." And Ringo just kind of grunted; it seemed okay to him, too. But nobody got up to make the call, and the moment passed. Still, when you think about it, it would have been pretty cool to go down in history as the guy who brought the Beatles back together.

4

The Producer

My father once told me: "There's great dignity in flipping burgers if you know you're going to own the joint one day."

The reason those words resonated for me at the time, after all those years, was because I was suddenly desperate to get out of session work. Every time I began to despair, however, another interesting person would pop into my life: the guys from Lynyrd Skynyrd, Tommy Bolin, Sheena Easton, Chaka Khan—more people than I can remember.

It was through these many sessions that I met Joe Gottfried, a lovely guy who had a studio in Van Nuys, and who decided to take a gamble on me as a producer. I don't know how that came about, exactly, but I think we were sitting around talking one night, and I told him I was ready to produce. He was surprised, as I remember it, because at that point I was pretty much near the top of the session game, but I told him I had this theory that all the smart people, in just about every walk of life (business, sports, entertainment, etc.), tended to get out while they were on top, or at least *near* the top, because they knew when it was time to move on. I'm not saying I was one of the smart ones, but I was definitely ready to produce.

"Unfortunately," I told Joe, "nobody's exactly clamoring for my services."

Around the same time a high-end keyboard maker developed something he called the "David Foster Sound." At the push of a button, it combined acoustic piano with electric piano. That was pretty flattering, but I *still* wanted to produce.

Joe was friendly with Jaye P. Morgan, an actress and singer, and he really believed in her talent. Knowing that I'd be able to bring some great musicians to the table, he offered me $5,000 to produce her debut album. I knew it would take me about six months, so I'd be taking a big financial hit, but sometimes you have to gamble on yourself.

For the next few months, working with some of the best session players in the business, I lived, ate, and breathed Jaye P.'s album.

She was wonderful, but the album did absolutely no business. Looking back, I'm sure it was overproduced, but I was genuinely happy with the results, and—more important—so were both Jaye P. and Joe Gottfried. At the end of the day, despite the fact that the album was a commercial failure, it set me off on the road to becoming a record producer.

From this experience, I learned another lesson: *Keep the blinders on—the road to success is straight, not full of curves.* Some people might say that this is not a good approach, and that it keeps you from seeing the world's myriad possibilities, but it has always worked for me.

My next effort was with two kids, Tom and John Keane, who must have been about ten or twelve years old. They sang pop, and they were super-talented, but that album didn't go anywhere either, and they went off to do a short-lived variety show for CBS.

I followed that up by producing Bill Champlin's first solo album, *Single*, with the help of my new engineering partner, Humberto Gatica, and that also bombed.

At that point, as you might imagine, I started getting really discouraged—almost as discouraged as I'd become toward the end of that crushingly lonely year in London. I was beginning to wonder whether I was cut out for producing. I thought I understood the job, and I thought I was doing everything a producer is supposed to do: Choose the musicians, make decisions about the material, guide the performances (both instrumental and vocal), help put the mix together, and deliver a finished record to the record company. But it just wasn't working. I'd done that on three albums in a row and all three had tanked.

And it's funny, because people often ask me what it takes to be a great producer, and I always give them the same answer. "It takes only one thing: an undying love of music."

In my case, it helps that I can play piano, along with half a dozen other instruments; that I can compose for orchestra; that I know how to arrange and write songs. But none of that is as important as the love of music. A producer can hire an arranger and a programmer and a dozen session players—along with an entire philharmonic orchestra—but without a love of music, any type of music, he's never going to create anything that comes from his heart.

Remember that early lesson: *Always go with what you love.*

As for me, I happen to produce middle-of-the-road music because I love it. And while the critics have not always been generous (understatement!), it seems that—more often than not—I have my finger on the pulse of what people want to hear.

That came later, of course. Much later. At that point in my career, almost thirty years ago now, I had produced three albums and was zero for three. I was making absolutely no money and was filled with doubt, as I had been many years earlier, as a kid in London, despairing about my chances of making it. And in fact there was a moment, maybe only a *fraction* of a moment, when I thought I should go back to session work. But I resisted. In my heart, I knew I could produce successfully, and I couldn't do that if I kept working as a studio musician. So I did what I had to do: I believed in myself almost to a point of madness.

Then I heard from Sonny Bono, whom I'd met at the Record Plant years earlier, and whom I'd played with, very briefly, when he went out on his own and needed a piano player. "I'm recording one last song with Cher," he told me.

"Really?" I said, dubious. "That's great." I was surprised, though. His marriage to Cher had broken up three years earlier, in 1974, and their musical partnership had died with it. Cher had since taken up with Greg Allman, and I believe Sonny was with Susie Coelho. Still, it *was* Sonny and Cher, so the potential for a big hit was there.

"I want you to be my arranger," Sonny said.

"Well, I'm really not that interested in being an arranger," I replied. "But if you let me co-produce it with you, I'll be happy to arrange it."

"You've got a deal," Sonny said.

This was a big moment for me. Huge, in fact. I was going to be co-producing a song with a pair of established professionals.

In the days ahead, Sonny and I worked together to make it happen. On the day Cher was scheduled to show up, I did the instrumental track and teed everything up so that we could get started the minute she walked into the studio. Sonny was as excited as a little kid. "She's going to be here in fifteen minutes," he said. "This is going to be great!" And five minutes later, "She's going to be here in ten minutes. This is going to be great!"

Cher showed up right on time, a true professional, but she was carrying attitude. Sonny tried to introduce her to me but she didn't seem interested. She strutted across the room, removed her jacket, and snapped, "Let's get this over with." My heart sank. *Let's get this over with?* I had really been looking forward to this. I'd been almost as excited as Sonny.

The song was called "You're Not Right For Me." Cher did two takes, then blew the joint. She hadn't so much as glanced in my general direction (though in years to come this great lady become a terrific friend). It was the last place she wanted to be, it was the last song she wanted to sing, and Sonny was clearly the last guy on the planet she wanted anything to do with.

"Well, that was interesting," I said.

"Yeah," Sonny said.

On the heels of that experience, I found myself working with Alice Cooper, who knew me as a session player but decided I had the makings of a producer. He was an unusual and impressive guy. Every morning, Alice would get out of bed, have breakfast with his kids, kiss his wife good-bye, drive the kids to school, play a round of golf, then show up at the studio and work his ass off with me, and that night he'd be at the arena in front of ten thousand fans, decapitating chickens.

Some of his earlier songs, like "Only Women Bleed" and "School's Out," were truly amazing, with incredible chord patterns. He was working with Dick Wagner and Bob Ezrin at the time, two very talented producers. The stuff he did with me was not his best, but we had fun doing it, and we had one Top 10 hit, "How Are You Gonna See Me Now," with Steve Lukather on guitar. Steve was eighteen at the time, and this was one of his first big breaks, and he did a big, raunchy solo that turned out very well.

Overall, though, I don't think I was edgy enough for Alice—but he never complained. I wasn't happy, though. This was 1978, and I'd been in Los Angeles for almost eight years, and in my hoped-for career as a producer I was now zero for four. Worse still, my marriage had fallen apart, and B.J. had moved into a nearby apartment with Amy, who was already five years old.

I went back to the house in North Hollywood and tried to make sense of my life. My youngest sister, Jaymes, was living with me, and she had just landed a job with Rocket Records, Elton John's old label. "You know," I told her. "B.J. and I have been separated for three months, and this is the longest period in my adult life I've been alone."

"How do you like it?" she asked.

"Not very much," I replied. I didn't realize that this would be my last period of singlehood for the next thirty years. If I had, maybe I'd have taken advantage of it.

Another one of my sisters, Marylou, was also living in Los Angeles. She was married to Ian Eales, a fellow Canadian who had always wanted to be in the music business, and some months earlier, when they'd been in town visiting, I invited them to dinner with my friend Jay Graydon, whom I'd met early in my session days. Jay did everything—he wrote songs, played guitar, arranged, produced—and I thought my brother-in-law might want to meet this immensely talented guy.

In the middle of dinner, Jay suddenly started turning blue. I was sitting beside him, so I stood up and began pounding him on the back, which is apparently the exact wrong thing to do. But my brother-in-law, one of those guys who knows a great deal about everything, leapt over the table, lifted Jay to his feet, and performed a flawless Heimlich maneuver, saving his life.

As soon as Jay's breathing returned to normal, he turned to look at Ian and Marylou. "I need to ask you something," he said. "How would you feel about moving to Los Angeles and coming to work for me." They moved down within a month, and for the next two decades they were in the music business together. That was great for me. I now had two sisters living close to me in Los Angeles.

Meanwhile, just as I was beginning to wonder whether I'd ever find another woman, a woman I could actually fall in love with, fate stepped in. I dropped in on a friend of mine, unannounced, and a woman answered the door. My friend wasn't around, but she was very attractive, so I stayed and we talked for a while. Her name was Rebecca. She lived in New York and worked as a flight attendant for American Airlines, and she asked me to look her up the next time I went east. Apparently, my friend was really into her, and eager to pursue a relationship, but—luckily for me—Rebecca didn't feel the same way about him.

Within a month, I found myself producing an album for Hall & Oates. As luck would have it, we were recording some of the tracks in New York, and I immediately called Rebecca, and from the first moment we got together we were inseparable.

I got the Hall & Oates job through David Paich, the brilliant leader of Toto, and he introduced me to Tommy Mottola, who was then a manager. Mottola had the demeanor of a gangster. One night he took me to dinner in Little Italy. The owner of the restaurant escorted us into the kitchen, to the prize table, and for the next three hours we were treated like visiting royalty. Mottola was not a big guy, but he exuded confidence, and he always walked into a room like he owned it. I got the distinct impression that he'd be running the world someday.

When my New York gig ended, Rebecca ended up coming back to Los Angeles with me, and I moved her into the house I'd once shared with B.J.

Oops. For a guy who'd grown up with six sisters, you'd think I would have known better.

One day, I came home from work to find four police cars and a fire truck out front, and of course I immediately panicked. It turned out that B.J. had come over to the house and become embroiled in a very loud and somewhat physical argument with Rebecca. As soon as I determined that Rebecca was okay, I began looking around for my assistant, a very sweet gay guy. I found him in a closet, where he'd been hiding ever since he made the call to 9-1-1.

On the heels of this, early in 1978, B.J. took Amy and moved to Toronto. I really didn't know how to be a long-distance dad, but I tried to be involved by calling Amy at least once a week and by sending money to provide for her and her mother. The rest of the time, I worked—I lost myself in my work.

At the time, I was again working with my friend Jay Graydon, but one day I got a call from Berry Gordy, the founder of Motown Records, and I went in to talk to him about Jaye P. Morgan's unreleased album. He liked it, but he had some ideas of his own. "It's good, real good," he said, "but you need to do something that combines both pop and R&B."

"I have something like that," I lied. I sat down at the piano and it was one of those moments where the chorus for the song just poured out of me like a gift from heaven: *Oh woh woh after the love has gone / What used to be right is wrong.* I remember thinking, *Goddamn it! This is great!* I couldn't believe that had come out of me on the spot and under pressure.

I raced back to the studio and burst in on Graydon. "Look what I came up with in Berry Gordy's office!" I said, and I sat down and played it for him. He loved it, too, and that became "After the Love Has Gone."

Yet another lesson: The best stuff comes *through* you, not *from* you. In that moment of panic in Berry Gordy's office, magic happened.

Anyway, Graydon and I worked on the song with Bill Champlin, who did the lyrics, and we played it for my friend Carol Childs, who knew Maurice White.

"David, this is a Number One song, and I am going to make you a promise," Carol told me. "I am going to get Maurice White to listen to it."

Now, as you may recall, Maurice White was the founder and front-man for that great R&B band, Earth, Wind & Fire, one of my all-time favorite bands. And as you may also recall, Earth, Wind & Fire was the *only* band on the planet that had earned the admiration of the hard-to-please Donny Gerrard, our singer from the Skylark days.

I went home and told Rebecca about it, and she could see how excited I was, but unlike B.J., who knew and understood music, and who would have recognized its significance immediately, this didn't really register for her in a significant way. But she was happy for me and incredibly supportive, and I couldn't really ask for more.

Not two weeks later, I went off to meet Maurice White at the Sunset Sound Studios, on Sunset Boulevard, in Hollywood. I was incredibly nervous. I desperately wanted to work with Maurice, partly because I was a huge fan, partly because I was desperate for a hit, and partly because I wanted Donny Gerrard to see that he had missed the boat with me. I'm not saying that Donny was a bad guy, mind you, but everybody needs a little stroking from time to time, and it would have been nice if, in the course of our many years together, he had said *one* kind word about my talents. Still, in a strange way, his indifference turned out to be a good thing. My desire to impress him—even if I never saw him again—turned out to be a real motivating force.

When I arrived at Sunset Sound, Maurice and his band were rehearsing, but he told the guys to take a break and I went in to see him. He was a charming guy, very friendly, and he immediately put me at ease. I guess he had experience with nervous white guys.

"So I hear you got a song for me," he said.

"Yes," I said. "I believe I do."

"You want to play it?"

"Now?" I said.

"Now would be a good time," he said, smiling.

I sat down at the piano, took a deep breath, and hit the keys. I even sang it for him, if you can believe it. Pretty much I suck as a singer.

When the song was over, he studied me for the longest time, then smiled and said, "I'd like to record that song." And he wasn't done with me yet. "I want to write some more songs with you," he went on. "When do you think you might have a little time?"

I couldn't believe this was happening to me. It was like a scene from a cheesy movie. A beam of light comes down from the heavens and lifts you up.

"I can be available," I said, and at that moment I knew, unequivocally, that abandoning session work had been one of the great decisions of my life (so far).

"Good," he said. "I'll be in touch."

A couple of weeks later I made the drive up to Maurice's spectacular 12-acre spread in Carmel. I arrived in the early evening, and within twenty minutes I was sitting at the piano and he was singing, and we were recording everything on one of those little cassettes.

At one point we took a break and Maurice offered me something to eat, but it looked like twigs and sticks. I didn't know what it was, but I knew Maurice was sort of a health freak, and I didn't want any part of it. I lost interest in eating and asked him if I could smoke in his pristine house. "I can't work without smoking," I said.

Maurice shook his head—he hated the idea of anyone smoking in his house—but we were making music together, and things were happening, so he made an exception and went off to find a small saucer I could use as an ashtray. "Man, you got to take care of your body," he said.

I had no interest in taking care of my body. "I smoke three packs of Marlboros a day, and my idea of a good meal is a hot dog or a grilled cheese sandwich with a double order of fries," I told him.

"How do you stay so skinny, then?"

He had a point. In those days, despite my six-foot frame, I weighed only 136 pounds, and my arms were so thin that I refused to wear short-sleeved shirts. (I once walked into a sauna and a half-naked stranger looked up at me, startled, and said, "Did you have pleurisy as a kid?")

Maurice was absolutely appalled by my diet, not to mention the cloud of smoke that followed me around, but the work was going well—and that's what mattered. I would sit at the piano and come up with a little something, and Maurice pretty much gave me free rein. That was part of his genius, the fact that he was open to absolutely everything. There were no boundaries. I could play jazz, classical, blues, or R&B—all the stuff I'd picked up by age sixteen, thanks to my teachers: Catherine Dash, Bob Bergeson, Rick Reynolds, Chuck Berry, Bo Diddley—and Maurice always found something positive to say about everything he heard.

At one point I drove into town for a hamburger, and left Maurice back at the house, working on some melodies, and not long after I got back things really started clicking. This went on for twelve hours straight, right through till seven the next morning, and we ended up writing a rough version of eight of the ten songs on the album in that one night. That was the *I Am* album, which went on to sell millions and millions of copies.

Still another lesson to think about: The best stuff often emerges full-blown. That night it certainly did.

In the months ahead, Maurice worked on some additional lyrics with the multitalented songwriter Allee Willis, and then we went into the studio to put the finishing touches on the work we'd done. I learned a lot from Maurice, and not all of it was about music.

One time, for example, in the middle of a recording session, we were working with the horns. Every single one of the horn players was black, and we were moving right along—until I stepped up to the podium at one point and said, in all innocence, "Okay, boys, let's take it from the top."

A moment later, I felt Maurice's hand on my arm. He led me into the Xerox room, which was not much bigger than a closet, and I'll never forget this. "Don't ever say 'boys' again," he said.

"I'm sorry," I said, unaware of the fact that my words could have been so easily misconstrued. "I didn't mean anything by it."

"I know you didn't, because I know you, but those guys don't know you, and they're all old-school. They might not like it."

"It won't happen again," I promised.

"Don't sweat it, man," he said. "I just don't want you to use that expression again because there's more history there than you could possibly understand."

"I'll be more careful," I said, still trying to understand what I'd done wrong.

"That's cool, man."

He treated me with such gentleness and tact that I loved him for it. But the incident really made me think: The notion that I might have struck anyone as even remotely racist had never crossed my mind. I grew up on an island in Canada. I didn't see my first black person till I was sixteen, when I moved to England, and I didn't have a racist bone in my body. Hell, I met my first *Jewish* person on that trip to England, and I had no idea what that even meant.

A week later, I was back in the studio with Maurice and the guys, hammering away at the piano, feeling good about the music and about life in general. I was isolated from the rest of the guys to keep the sound of their instruments from leaking into mine, only this time I was somewhat more isolated than usual. I was off in a distant corner, with a curtain separating me from the rest of the players, but didn't think much of it. Sometimes you use big towels to muzzle the sound; they'd opted for a curtain. And it wasn't a problem, anyway. We were all wearing headphones; we didn't need to be on top of each other. Later, though, the guys in the band started pulling my leg. "Did you know that *Jet* magazine was here to do an interview with us?" one of them said.

"No, I didn't know that," I replied.

"Why do you think we hid you behind that curtain?"

"I thought I was behind the curtain to keep the sound from leaking," I said.

"No," another guy said. "You were behind the curtain because this is an R&B group, and you're the first white guy who ever worked with us, a little white guy from Canada, and we don't want the folks at *Jet* magazine to find out about you."

They were just jiving, though. And we had a good laugh about it. I knew Maurice White wasn't hiding me. I might have been white, but I had enough funk in me to work with Earth, Wind & Fire. Hell, I actually co-wrote "Got to Be Real" for Cheryl Lynn, a huge R&B hit. (My first ex-wife is still living off royalties from that song.) How could anyone even suggest I was too white?

Strangely enough, I remember running into Maurice again a few years later. I was producing something for Kenny Rogers at the time, and I told Maurice about it, and he turned to me and said, "You know, I never get called for any of those jobs."

"Are you kidding?" I said. "With your track record!"

"No," he said. "I don't get called for that stuff."

And when I thought about it later, I understood what he meant. He mostly produced for black acts. And I think that's a pity, because every single group on the planet that's doing any kind of funk at all owes a huge debt to Maurice White.

In my life, James Brown wasn't the godfather; Maurice White was.

It was thanks largely to that relationship with Maurice that in 1979 I won my first Grammy for "After the Love Has Gone." The song made it all the way to Number Two on the pop charts, kept from the top spot by the Knack's "My Sharona." The three worst spots on the chart are Number 2, Number 6, and Number 11: the first because it keeps you from being the Number One song, and the other two because they keep you out of the Top 5 and the Top 10.

Still, I'm not complaining. Winning a Grammy is about the greatest thing that can happen to a musician. It's our version of the Oscar.

Rebecca and I went to the ceremonies together, but this wasn't a category the network bothered to televise. (Some ninety Grammys are handed out each year, but the network covers only about a dozen.) It was still pretty exciting, though. They called our names—Bill Champlin, Jay Graydon, and me—and we went up to collect the Grammy for "Best Rhythm & Blues Song."

As soon as we left the stage, I ran outside and stood in line at a phone booth and called my mother in Victoria. I was over the moon with excitement, and I kept trying to impress upon her how much this meant to me. I was so wired I'm not sure I gave her a chance to get a word in, then I hurried back to rejoin Rebecca at our seats, walking on air.

I went home that night feeling a great sense of belonging. I don't know how else to put it. I was part of the music industry. As I had told my mother, *I'd just been anointed by my peers.*

But the next morning, I put my pants on, like a regular guy—"one leg at a time," as my mother used to say—and went off to Jerry's Deli to have breakfast with Rebecca. I walked inside and actually had to wait a few minutes for a table, *like everybody else.* Bummer.

About a minute after we sat down, I started getting incredible chest pains. I thought for sure I was having a heart attack, and that I was on the verge of death, and Rebecca managed to get me into the car—with the help of a couple of nervous waiters—and drove me to the hospital. On our way there, all sorts of crazy thoughts were running through my head: *This is God talking to you, David. You've smoked three packs a day since you were thirteen, and now you're going to die like a fucking idiot, without your breakfast even. But you got your Grammy, right? Like that's gonna save your ass!*

I couldn't believe it. Not twelve hours after winning my first

Grammy, I was being wheeled into the emergency room. *Is that how the universe works?* I wondered. *Is the universe really that cruel?* I figured that was as good a time as any to make a pact with God: *If you let me live,* I promised, *I will never, ever, smoke another cigarette again for as long as I walk the earth.*

For the next few hours, the doctors subjected me to one test after another, and—except for a little heart murmur, which I'd known about since I was a kid—they found me to be in perfect health. It seemed I'd had a minor anxiety attack, nothing more. I was tempted to break my word to God—it wasn't a heart attack, so maybe it didn't count—but I prevailed and went cold turkey that very morning. It was much harder than I'd imagined. I couldn't get out of bed for two days. I refused to talk to anyone. I wouldn't even answer the phone. But one day, the dark cloud lifted, and I felt magically transformed, and I got up and went back to work.

The period that followed turned into a dizzying, nonstop hit-making tear. They would just slide the food under the studio door and I'd keep producing music. Poor Rebecca. All I cared about was making music.

Not all of it came easy, though. I remember working with Boz Scaggs at the time, on "Look What You've Done to Me," for the *Urban Cowboy* soundtrack, and it struck me as one of the toughest assignments I'd ever had. We were in my little house in North Hollywood, the one I shared with Rebecca, and I sat there for three hours, trying different things on the piano. Boz gave me nothing. And I mean, *nothing.* He was the polar opposite of Maurice White. He fiddled with his pencil and paper, nodding and tapping his foot from time to time, and it wasn't until many hours later, when I *finally* hit a chord he liked, that he suddenly came alive: "That's it!" he shouted. "That's what we want! Let's work on that."

We finished it in the space of the afternoon, recorded it the next morning, and that was it. Signed, sealed, and delivered. "Look What You've Done to Me" became a Top 10 hit, so it was well worth it: another notch in the belt. I love Boz.

Another memorable experience during this very productive period was a result of my work with the Average White Band, but it was only indirectly related to them. Some years earlier, during the session years, I had met Quincy Jones, the legendary music impresario, and I think that—in some small way—I was on his radar. So I decided to show him some of the "great" work I'd done with the Average White Band, partly because I was looking for his approval, and partly to show him that I was moving up in the world.

"Skip over track two," I said, handing him the album. "It's no good. Forget about four and five—the vocals are out of tune. Track six, well—they wanted that one, not me."

Quincy took the album from me and asked, "What does it say right here?"

"Says 'Average White Band'."

"No, jackass, *here*." He was pointing at my name.

"It says, 'Produced by David Foster'."

"Right. And listen to the excuses you're making. Either it's exactly the way you think it should be, or don't put your name on it."

At that moment, the light bulb went on, and I realized that—right or wrong—I needed to be in control of my destiny. I was never going to compromise again. And I learned that important lesson from Quincy Jones: *Compromise breeds mediocrity.*

From that day forward, I have always fought for my artistic vision. I don't always win, but I always do my best. At the end of the day, it's about sticking to your creative instincts. Of course, that has created a few problems for me along the way, and the rap on David Foster is that he's a control freak. But guess what? I can live with that. And the reason I can live with it is because I always give 110 percent. Every day, day after day. When someone hires me as a producer, it is my job to push him or her toward greatness. I'm not saying that I *make* them great, but I often manage to coax an extra five or ten percent out of them—by guiding, encouraging, persisting—that makes them *reach* for greatness. My goal is to get more out of artists than anybody else they've ever worked with in their lives.

I will also do anything to make my artists happy, of course—a glass of water, a rest, fresh flowers, a backrub—but I do it with ulterior motives: *to get things out of them that they didn't know were there.* Am I tough on them sometimes? Yes. Is it worth it? Definitely.

A case in point:

As the eighties got underway, I was making quite a name for myself as a producer, and one day I got a call about going to work for Chicago, a band I'd always loved. I'd been up for a producing gig with them a couple of years earlier, in the pre-Grammy days—thanks to manager Jeff Wald, whom I'd met through Helen Reddy—but it didn't happen because they didn't think I had enough experience. Some months earlier, I had a similar experience with Julio Iglesias. I went to meet him at Sony, hoping to get the job, and he took one look at me and shook his head. "You seem like a nice guy, and I think you're talented," he said. "But no—you're too young."

But here we were, a couple of years later, and Chicago had moved on to their next album, *Chicago 16.* My name came up again, and the guys figured I was a little older and a little wiser, so they took a vote. It wasn't unanimous, but I was in, and I was absolutely thrilled. When I first heard the band, back in 1969, I was living in Edmonton, and I loved everything about it—the horns, the rhythm, the drums, the great vocals. If I had to choose two CDs to take with me to a desert island, one would be by Chicago and the other would be by Blood, Sweat & Tears.

Anyway, on my first day of work I arrived at a big place in the San

Fernando Valley, the home of Danny Serafine, the drummer, and I listened patiently as they played the thirteen songs they intended to use on the new album.

I sat there, nodding my head and tapping my feet, Boz Scaggs-style, and when it was over I looked up and found all of them staring at me, waiting for my reaction. "Guess what?" I said. "You guys are my favorite band. I've been a fan since 1969, when you were calling yourself Chicago Transit Authority, but these songs suck. If I'm going to produce this album, we're going to have to write thirteen new songs, because this isn't even close to what you should be doing."

It took balls to say that, but I'd learned my lesson from Quincy Jones. My name was going to be on that album. These guys had forgotten their greatness, and my job, in part, was to remind them of that greatness.

I know my harsh response was a bit of a shock to them—when you're creating, you always think you're doing great work—and they pissed and moaned for a while, but before long they got over it and we rolled up our sleeves and went to work.

At the end of the day, the fact that I was such a fan was a huge boon to them. I knew some of their horn licks better than they did, and I spent much of my time trying to recreate their greatest moments. I had done the same with Earth, Wind & Fire—basically stealing from their own best stuff, which is what made it work.

I spent the better part of a year going to their various houses, and they were very difficult. They always had meetings. They had meetings about meetings. But eventually we came up with thirteen new songs, most of which were written by Peter Cetera, the lead vocalist, and me. I liked Peter. I also liked Jimmy Pankow, the trombone player, because he's a great musician, and he was very much responsible for their sound, but I got the distinct feeling that Pankow wasn't all that wild about me.

Peter also had some problems with me, perhaps finding me a little too blunt. This stemmed from one of our first days in the studio, when he made a mistake on the bass and I corrected him. "Peter," I said, "right before we get to the bridge, it's not a C, it's a D"—or whatever the hell it was. And he looked at me, glanced at the guys—who looked like they were getting ready for the shit to hit the fan—then put down his bass and motioned with his finger. I followed him out and I had a feeling I was heading into the Xerox room again. I was right. As soon as we were out of earshot he turned to face me and said, "Please don't ever correct me in front of the band again."

"I'm sorry," I said, but I didn't really mean it.

"And you know," he went on, "now that I think about it, I don't even want to play bass. You're good with synthesizer bass. Why don't *you* take over?"

This was wonderful news! Peter was a good bass player, but letting me take over gave me that much more control over the album. I also ended up playing piano, because their regular piano payer, the talented Bobby Lamb, was unavailable. I also played Moog bass, something I'd learned from Gary Wright when we were making *The Dream Weaver,* and I'd like to think I made a significant contribution to the album's sound. No, I *know* I made a significant contribution to their sound. I don't give a shit what they say. I know what I did: I was the piano player, the bass player, the arranger, the co-songwriter, and the producer.

Peter was pretty intense, and everyone tended to walk on eggshells when he was around, but it was worth it. We wrote some real classics together, including "Love Me Tomorrow," "Stay the Night," "Hard To Say I'm Sorry," and "You're the Inspiration."

I also worked on the band's next two albums, and those three albums combined sold upward of ten million copies. The album that preceded them sold a grand total of 110,000 units. Enough said?

Years later, long after Peter left Chicago, we teamed up on the Oscar-nominated theme song "Glory of Love," for *The Karate Kid,*

Part II. We challenged each other on that project, as we'd done on every other project, but it was worth it. Peter is one of my all-time favorite singers and a great talent. And I'll go back to what I said earlier: *Compromise breeds mediocrity*. If I want the note to go an octave higher, and you want the note to go an octave lower, and we meet in the middle—well, we both lose.

I don't care if people think I'm a control freak. That's part of the job description. You've got to fight for what you believe in. That's what I did back then, and that's what I do to this day.

5

Slip Sliding Away

After I finished working on that first Chicago album, I was completely drained. Those guys could drive you crazy with their meetings, and their meetings about meetings, endlessly analyzing every little riff and lick. And it got worse when we were actually recording. The singers would ask for more vocals and less horns, for example, and the horns would ask for more horns and less vocals, which led to more battles and more headaches.

I was sitting at home with Rebecca one afternoon, still recuperating, playing with our baby daughter, Sara, who'd come along in 1981, when I got a call from Ned Shankman, my manager at the time. "Paul McCartney is interested in working with you," he said.

I couldn't believe it. This was the guy who had changed my life with "She Loves You," and he was calling to see if I was available to help him on his next album.

Before I knew it, Rebecca and I flew to London, with Sara and Ned Shankman, and at one point, not an hour into our ten-hour flight, all hell broke loose. Ned was playing with little Sara, holding her up by the straps of her OshKosh baby overalls, when the strap broke and she fell to the floor of the plane. For a moment, she didn't utter a sound, and Ned reached for her before I could even unbuckle my seatbelt. By the time I had her in my arms, however, she was wailing. And she was covered in blood. One of her little teeth gone through her tiny lip, and it was gushing everywhere.

Finally, we got things under control. Poor Ned kept apologizing, and Rebecca and I kept telling him that it wasn't his fault, but we all felt like shit—and we were all exhausted by the time we landed.

The moment we walked into the hotel room I started sobbing. I don't know what was going on—maybe I was having a breakdown, maybe I was just completely burned out (the kind of burnout Kevin Costner had been talking about), or maybe it was the stress of having seen my daughter in that kind of pain—but I sat on the edge of the bed and wept for hours, and there was nothing Rebecca could do to make me stop. I finally cried myself to sleep, and in the morning I got up and went downstairs to wait for Paul McCartney.

He picked me up in this tiny little car, a Mini Cooper, and we drove over to his house. He didn't say much en route, and he didn't say much when we got there. He introduced me to Linda Eastman, his wife, and to two of the kids, and before I knew it we were jamming. It was like something out of *The Partridge Family*. Everyone picked up an instrument and started making music, just fooling around, having a good time, and it reminded me of jamming with my own dad.

The McCartneys lived in a simple, five-bedroom house. Nothing fancy. I remember a solitary sofa in the living room, in front of the TV, and two genuine Picassos leaning against a corner—which they apparently hadn't gotten around to hanging.

I also remember Linda making dinner for us at the end of that first day. She served us soy burgers at the kitchen table, right out of the frying pan. And after dinner one of the kids had to go to some function at school, a dance, I think, and he came running in and asked Paul if he could borrow his jacket. "Okay," Paul said. "But only if you promise to bring it back."

It was so normal as to appear surreal. I wanted something *different*. I don't know what, exactly, but this was Paul McCartney.

Unfortunately, Paul and I didn't click musically. I had gone to London thinking we were going to write "The Long and Winding Road, Part II," but that didn't happen. Maybe it was me. As I said, I was in pretty bad shape. But I don't think Paul was blameless. I loved the guy and I was still in awe of him, perhaps too much so, but I also felt that he was one of those musicians who needed to be reminded of his greatness. I tried, but he wasn't listening, and it was a little like being on a bad date. Or a series of bad dates—ten bad dates in a row, maybe. I kept hoping for something good to happen, for some kind of breakthrough, but we never got anywhere. In some ways it was a little difficult to give direction to someone I held in such high regard, and that problem was further compounded when Dave Gilmour showed up at the studio. Gilmour was Pink Floyd's brilliant guitarist, and I was too intimidated to give him any direction. I kept thinking, *How am I supposed to tell this guy what to do?* I didn't, of course. And that was a mistake.

I compromised, breaking my own rule, and it showed in the results.

One day, right near the end of our time together, during yet another typically dark and rainy afternoon the recording desk broke down and the technician told us it would take at least a couple of hours to fix it. Paul and I went off to the studio kitchen and had a seat, and he looked across at me. "Looks like we've got at least two hours," he said. "Ask me anything you like."

I couldn't believe this was happening. I was as excited as a little kid. I was finally going to get The Truth, and I was going to hear it from the man himself.

The thing I was most curious about was the day the Beatles broke up, but I decided I should ease my way into it, so I began by asking him about George Harrison, since I'd worked with him and knew him a little.

"What do you want to know about George?" Paul said.

"He was an *amazing* songwriter, wasn't he? I mean, 'Something' is truly one of the greatest songs of all time."

Paul flashed a sly grin. "Well, I suppose everybody's got *one* in 'em."

I thought he was kidding, and maybe he was. Then again, maybe he wasn't—maybe the press had got it wrong from the start: Maybe the rub wasn't John and Paul, as everyone assumed, but *George* and Paul. I could have dug a little, and asked him to explain further, but I'm not sure I wanted to know.

Finally, I got around to asking him about the breakup—the one question every Beatle aficionado has been asking from the beginning of the end, and probably the most overanalyzed moment in music history—and he was pretty blunt about that, too. He said the band had scheduled a meeting, and John showed up late, with Yoko Ono at his side. He turned to the three others and said, "I'm quitting the band." That's all he said. Then he and Yoko turned around and marched out.

"Then what happened?" I said, on the edge of my seat.

"Well," Paul replied, "we did what every other band would do under similar circumstances. We turned to each other and said, 'Who can we get?' And we started thinking about possibilities. Clapton. Beck. Richards."

I believed him. As any kid who has ever been in a similar situation will confirm, when one of the band members bails on you those are always the first words out of your mouth: *Who can we get?*

A few months after we returned from London, we bought a nice house in Toluca Lake, and before we were quite settled in I had to leave for New York. I spent almost three months there, producing the soundtrack to *Dreamgirls,* for which I won another Grammy, but the thing I remember most about that trip is the fact that I developed claustrophobia, particularly when it came to elevators. In two successive days, in two separate places, I got stuck in an elevator. The first was at the Parker Meridien Hotel, where I was staying, and the second was at the legendary Dakota, on West 72nd Street, where I was visiting Roberta Flack (and where John Lennon would be murdered in 1980). Neither incident lasted more than a few minutes, but when I emerged from the elevator at the Dakota I was completely freaked out.

The best way I can describe it—and you'll relate to this only if you're a parent—is that feeling you get when you're in the supermarket or the hardware store or wherever and you turn around and for a moment your child is nowhere in sight: a panic so intense it's almost impossible to put into words. I was so traumatized, in fact, that I told myself I would never again set foot in an elevator. And I never did. *Willingly.* But more on that later.

When I got back to Los Angeles, I really began hitting my stride. I did *Chicago 17* and *Chicago 18* with my engineer, Humberto—more meetings, more madness—and I worked with both Kenny Loggins and Kenny Rogers. Whatever had happened to me in that hotel in

London, breakdown or not, was well behind me. For the next couple of years, I was firing on all eight cylinders.

Erin, our second daughter, came along in 1982, and I was thrilled to death. I'd grown up with six sisters, and I loved women, so I told Rebecca to please keep having daughters.

Among the many people I worked with over the course of the next couple of years, I especially remember Lionel Richie, and the many hours we spent locked away in the studio on *Can't Slow Down*. I loved working with Lionel, but he did a terrible thing to me. I called his house at nine one morning and his then-wife, Brenda, heard my voice and gasped. "Oh my God, David! Are you all right?" I didn't know what she was talking about, but I somehow bluffed my way through it, and the gist of it was that I had had a heart attack, and that Lionel had spent the night next to my bed at Cedars-Sinai, practically holding my hand. I don't know where Lionel had spent the night, and I don't know if he ever cheated on his wife, but he was a smart guy, and you'd think he could have come up with a more viable alibi.

In February 1985, the year Jordan was born—my third daughter with Rebecca—Lionel and I won the Grammy for Producer of the Year. Rebecca and I attended the ceremony together, as did Lionel and his wife, and they brought a friend with them, Linda Thompson. I noticed her right away—she was very striking—and later that night I talked to her at the Grammy party, which was held at Le Dome, on Sunset Boulevard. I learned that she had recently separated from Bruce Jenner, the 1976 Olympic decathlon champ, and that they had two small boys, Brandon and Brody, who were four and two at the time.

A week later, Rebecca and I were at Lionel's house, and there she was again. We were chatting, and Rebecca and I told her that we were thinking of moving to Malibu, and Linda said, "You should come by my house. I'd love to show you around town."

And that's when it all began, a very difficult period in my life: Linda and I started an affair. Everything about it was wrong, and it was unforgivable on every level, and there's absolutely nothing I can say in my defense. Rebecca was a great homemaker and a wonderful mother to our three beautiful girls, but I seemingly had no respect for the sanctity of marriage—even if it *had* lost some of its spark. I couldn't understand it, but it didn't stop me from destroying the life that Rebecca and I had built together. How had I turned into such a complete asshole?

Despite the drama, Linda and I tried to make things work as a blended family. We had all the kids together on weekends—six kids between us, ages five, five, four, three, one, and twelve (Amy, my daughter with B.J.)—and we took them on ski trips and other vacations, but right from the start these outings become a source of friction, not of joy. Like any divorced parent, I was in regular contact with both Rebecca and B.J., for updates on the girls, and Linda seemed inexplicably threatened by this. Eventually, instead of putting my foot down and establishing some rules, I began to see less and less of my daughters, and to this day that is my single greatest regret. Why is it that wisdom always comes too late and at an advanced age? (I heard a great line once: "It takes seventy years to make a man, and then he's only good for dying.")

Linda and I eventually stopped arguing about the girls, and about my exes, but the guilt was overwhelming—and I dealt with it by doing what many good workaholics do: I lost myself in my music. In the studio, there was escape. Amid all this turmoil, I won my third and fourth Grammys for my work with Chicago and Peter Cetera, one for Producer of the Year and another for Best Instrumental Accompanying Vocals ("Hard Habit to Break").

Then I went back to work with Barbra Streisand. She was dating Richard Baskin at the time, a friend of mine, and he thought I would be the perfect guy to produce "Somewhere." That opinion was wholeheartedly endorsed by Barbra's longtime manager, the terrific Marty Erlichman, who called and urged me to take the job, but I was so busy

I couldn't bring myself to commit. Then Baskin offered me the one thing I can never say no to: private air travel. "If you do this for us," he said, "I will get you ten hours on the Time-Warner corporate jet."

When I arrived for our first session, at the A&M Studios in Hollywood, Barbra and I hugged and caught up. Then she said, "I want this song to sound like it was not created on this planet."

"I'll see what I can do," I said.

I ended up using only synthesizers to get a richly layered background—no orchestra at all—and I worked every day for a month, with seven different programmers, to get it right. This was going to be the cornerstone of the album, and it was our only real chance at a Number One hit.

The night I finished, I looked over at my engineer, Humberto, and told him I was going to call Barbra. I reached her at home and let her know we were done, and she was so anxious to hear it that she asked me to drive down to Malibu right away. It was a Saturday night, around ten o'clock, and it took us about forty-five minutes to get out to her place, and from the looks of all the fancy cars out front she was having a party. I rang the bell and Elizabeth Taylor opened the door. "Hello, yes, can I help you?" she said. She was wearing sequins and an evening gown. This was clearly a very highfalutin party—and I hadn't been invited!

"Yes," I said. I was in shock. I was dressed in jeans, and I'd been holed up in the studio for a month, so I'm not sure I was making a very good impression. "I'm, uh—I'm David Foster. Barbra asked me to stop by."

"Oh yes!" she answered. "You're the man who's bringing the music."

At that moment, Barbra showed up and whisked us through the house, and I remember seeing Clint Eastwood standing in a corner, chatting with some of the other A-list guests. Barbra took Humberto and me into her study and I played the song for her. She listened in silence, and when it was over she turned to me and said, "I love it. I absolutely love it!"

I have to tell you, in all modesty, it was spectacular. Barbra's description had pushed me to create something otherworldly, and that's exactly what it sounded like—like music that had been created on another planet. I won my fifth Grammy for that song.

That same year, I scored the movie *St. Elmo's Fire*—I'd produced songs for *Footloose* and *Ghostbusters*, and would continue to work on other films (*Pretty Woman, Three Men and a Baby,* etc.)—but the *St. Elmo's* love theme, an instrumental, actually turned into a hit. And something very cool happened as a result. My friend Kenny Loggins was performing at the Santa Barbara Bowl, and he said to me, "Why don't you join me and play your song in the middle of my concert?" I thought that was an interesting and generous idea, so I agreed to do it.

On the big day, I was nervous as hell, and I got more nervous when I walked onto the stage and saw 5,000 people in the audience. But the moment I started playing, everyone burst into wild applause—not because I was so great, necessarily, but because they recognized the song—and I was instantly fueled by their enthusiasm. I remember thinking, *If this is what performing is all about, I love it—and I finally get it.* I told myself that I would have to figure out some way of performing from time to time, because I liked the feeling; I liked it a *lot*.

I then went off to produce a few songs for Olivia Newton-John, and we actually did a duet together (believe it or not). She was absolutely gorgeous, and neither of us was available, but my innocent crush on her added a nice energy to the work. After that, I did something I don't believe I had ever done in my entire adult life: I started taking some time off.

I still remember exactly how that started. It was a Sunday. I'd just had breakfast with Linda, and I was getting ready to go off to work when she said, "Why don't you just sit on the porch today and do nothing?"

This was a completely alien concept to me. Whenever people talked about taking the weekend off, I'd always assumed it meant not working on Saturday night. I had always worked all day Saturday, and all day Sunday, and I didn't think anyone really needed more than one night a week to kick back.

"Why would I want to do nothing?" I said.

And Linda said, "Because you work all the time. And you might enjoy it."

I had never really thought about it in those terms. I'm one of those lucky guys who discovered what he wanted to do with his life at a very early age, and I had never stopped doing it. Most kids, by the time they get to college, are probably more confused than ever about the future, but somehow they're expected to make a choice at age eighteen: *Maybe I should be a doctor. No, being a lawyer sounds more interesting. Or—if it's real excitement I'm looking for—I guess I could go to work for the C.I.A.* That's crazy to me; that's the reason most people end up doing what they're trained to do, not what they love doing, and I feel for them, because those kids don't have a dream. That was never an issue for me. I loved what I was doing, and I loved being busy. In fact, every time an interesting side project came along, I ended up doing it on weekends. I'd get a call from someone telling me they needed me to write or produce a song, and if I liked the sound of it I'd look for my next available opening and book it, and the few open slots I had tended to be on Saturdays and Sundays. That was the way I'd always operated. I couldn't say no to anything that piqued my interest. And often I couldn't even say no to anything that *didn't* pique my interest. My work was my life.

For some reason, however, I kicked back that Sunday, and it happened again the next Sunday, and the Sunday after that. And I honestly think it hurt me. No, I don't think it; I *know* it. I got off the treadmill. And I think I did this largely because I was in such a confused state. I was living in Malibu with Linda and her two boys, and I was seeing less and less of my girls, and the guilt wouldn't let up. In retrospect, I believe the pain and confusion are what led, perhaps indirectly, to my getting off the treadmill—and that's how I found myself kicking back on the porch.

I remember talking to composer Burt Bacharach about this, many years later, and he said to me, "I went to Palm Springs once for a two-week vacation and I stayed for two years. I didn't write, I didn't play music, I didn't do a thing." And I think that's what was starting to happen. I had taken my eye off the tiger, but I wasn't aware of it, *yet.*

Then the strangest thing happened. My mother called to tell me that there was a young girl from Victoria waiting for a liver transplant in a Los Angeles hospital. "Could you go visit her?" she said. "Just to say hello to the family. I'm sure it would make them feel better. They're from our hometown."

So I went, and it was probably one of the most intense experiences of my life. In the first bed, there was a beautiful little seven-year-old who'd been in a drowning accident and was for all intents and purposes brain-dead. Her parents were just waiting to pull the plug. In the next bed there was a boy who'd had a catastrophic fall, and it was clear he would never be the same again. And in the third bed I found the little girl from Victoria, Rachel. She was four years old and very, very sick, and I introduced myself to her and to her mother, and sat next to her bed. "If I could do one thing for you," I said, "anything at all, what would it be?" I expected her to ask for a Barbie doll, or a trip to Disneyland, but instead she said, "It's my sister's birthday pretty soon, and I really, really want to see her so I can wish her a happy birthday and give her a big hug." And something clicked for me at that moment. This little girl's sister was back in Victoria. For the price of a plane ticket, I could bring her to Los Angeles and make her greatest wish come true. And of course I immediately made arrangements to fly her down, and I returned to the hospital two days later for the reunion.

I cannot even begin to tell you what that moment did to me: Watching the little girl's face light up when her sister walked into the room brought me to tears. It's a moment that is absolutely beyond description.

On the drive home, it occurred to me that there must be hundreds and thousands of families in similar predicaments. I might not be able to cover their medical costs, but I thought I'd be able to help them with all the things most of us never even think about—travel, food, lodging, etc. They needed help managing the chaos their lives had become. There were hotel rooms to pay for, transportation to and from the hospital, meals, flights to and from their homes so they could take turns with their ailing children. I could help people like that. I could try to find them affordable apartments, buy them used cars, maybe even contribute to their mortgage payments while they took time off from work to focus on the only thing that really mattered at that point—their children.

I had young children of my own and I couldn't help but think of them. Maybe I thought that by helping other children it would make up for the things I wasn't doing for my own daughters; I'm not sure. All I know is that suddenly my own problems seemed insignificant.

Before the end of the year, I created the David Foster Foundation, and for the next three years we raised funds by organizing celebrity softball games in Victoria. Big names always turned up to entertain the fans. At the very first one, I managed to get Gene Hackman, John Travolta, Michael J. Fox, Wayne Gretzky, and Olivia Newton-John, among others, and I tried very hard to make it worth their while. I had them fly in a couple of days early, and I'd take them boating and swimming and arrange tennis games and put on a barbecue, and they'd all be glowing and happy by the weekend, when we put on the show. On

Monday, when it was time to say good-bye, nobody wanted to go home. They'd been having too much fun. And maybe that's one of the reasons they keep coming back to help me raise money.

I also remember that first event because I was out on the field one afternoon, after our celebrity softball game, signing autographs and pretending to be a big shot, when I heard a voice hollering at me from the stands. "Dave! Hey, Dave!" I looked up at a battered face that seemed vaguely familiar. "It's me! Gary Druce! Remember me?" I took a closer look. It really *was* him—the guy who used to torment me relentlessly at P.E. I went over to shake his hand, and the closer I got the worse he looked. This was clearly a guy who had fallen on hard times, and my heart went out to him. I invited him to the concert that night, and he sat next to me, and neither of us said a single word about our shared history. But I know he had a wonderful time, because he kept thanking me, and his presence made it a great night for me, too. He probably had no idea that he'd had such a dramatic effect on my life.

In the years since, the foundation has moved from softball games to concerts, sometimes as many as half a dozen a year, and we have raised tens of millions of dollars to help critically ill children and their families. I tell you this not because I'm a shameless self-promoter, which I might be, but because of how much it has done for me, personally. The truth is—and I know this is a cliché—you definitely get more out of giving than you put in. *Much* more.

I love music, and I will always love music, but the foundation was about saving lives. And that's it. There is nothing else.

I continue to put a lot of time, effort, and money into the foundation because it makes me feel good about myself. Period. The motivation is largely selfish. Also, beyond making me feel good, I'm a bit of a ham. As you may recall, about a year before my mother phoned to tell me about that little girl from Victoria, Kenny Loggins had asked me to perform at the Santa Barbara Bowl, an experience I found to be instantly addictive. And part of the reason I do these fundraisers is because I love to perform. The concerts give me a chance to feed that addiction. I may be the least impressive entertainer on the roster, but I enjoy being on stage. Plus I'm in charge—and I'm going to be up there playing the piano and hosting, whether the guests like it or not. And the fact of the matter is, I'm performing for free, so who's going to fire me?

Some years into the charity work, I met Marvin Davis, the oil billionaire, and his wife, Barbara. They had been running the annual Carousel of Hope Ball since 1978, to help children with diabetes, and at one point they asked me to help them organize the entertainment, which I've now done for them about a dozen times. That experience led to other fundraisers for other organizations. The Andre Agassi Charitable Foundation, which raises money for at-risk boys and girls; Muhammad Ali's Celebrity Fight Night, which helps fund Parkinson's research (two of my perennial favorites); Cedars-Sinai, the Race to Erase MS, and Starry, Starry Night for the Grammys, and—whatever it is—every minute I've spent on those projects makes me feel really good about myself. At this point fundraising consumes almost a third of my life, but it feeds me as an entertainer, and it does tangible good—and you can't beat that.

On a home front, Linda and I were trying to enjoy life, playing the role of the fun Hollywood couple, but my other life, my previous life, continued to be a source of tremendous friction. I never imagined it would be so hard to blend our two families. I wanted my daughters to love Linda, and I wanted Linda to love my daughters, but our relationship had gotten off to a terrible start—with infidelity—and it was the children who ended up paying for it. I wasn't seeing enough of them; I wasn't being enough of a father.

The heartache also affected me professionally, and I hit a rocky patch. Looking back I've come to believe that it was probably connected to the divorce and to my guilt over leaving my children, along with those first two years of almost endless disagreements with Linda. Don't get me wrong: I was still working, still making money, still being productive. But it wasn't the same.

I composed and recorded *The Symphony Sessions,* performing my own compositions with the eighty-three-piece Vancouver Symphony Orchestra. I toured Asia. I produced certain artists purely for money. I wrote and produced "Can't You Feel It," the official theme song of the Calgary 1988 Winter Olympics, with my friend Tommy Banks, the piano-playing senator from Edmonton. I did *River of Love* with contributions from Bryan Wilson, Natalie Cole, Bryan Adams, Bruce Hornsby, and Mike Reno. I teamed up with Neil Diamond on *The Best Years of Our Lives,* thinking we were making his big comeback album—I was convinced that "Carmelita's Eyes" was absolutely brilliant—and we fell way short.

As I said earlier, something simply wasn't clicking. I'm not sure if the rest of the music world noticed, but I certainly did. It was a brief period, admittedly—less than two years—but there were mornings when I got out of bed and felt like slashing my wrists. I feel I have to earn my value every day, and at that point I was feeling almost entirely devoid of value.

During this same period, a friend of mine in Canada, Carol Reynolds, then the head of CBC Television, sent me a tape of a French-Canadian singer, telling me she thought she was amazing. The tape was made at a televised event, some kind of singing contest, and I remember watching it with my engineer, Humberto, with whom I'd been working almost from the start. The girl opened her mouth and we couldn't believe what we were hearing. "This is insane," I said. "She *can't* be that good."

In fact, I was convinced she was lip-synching, because no one sounded that good live, and certainly not in a televised competition.

Some weeks later, however, I found out that she was performing north of Montreal, and I flew up to see if she was the real thing. We had to drive fifty miles through pouring rain, and we found ourselves in an open field where people had gathered for a picnic, taking cover from the rain under leaky tents.

The singer's name was Celine Dion, and she was under a tent of her own, and the moment she began to sing my whole world stopped. It was like something out of a movie, where I found myself suddenly transported by that voice. Celine and I were the only two people on the planet. She was *that* good. When I snapped out of it, I noticed that the rest of the crowd was hardly paying attention—they were drinking and eating—and it really pissed me off. I couldn't believe these people weren't listening. Didn't they know that they were witnessing greatness?

Celine performed a second song, and by the time she was done I honestly thought I had just heard the best singer on the planet, and I hurried over to introduce myself to her and to her manager, René Angélil. She had a record deal in Quebec, René informed me, and they were looking for an American connection.

"You just found it," I said, turning to look at Celine. "I want to bring you to America. You are absolutely astonishing." René translated for me, and Celine smiled and said in broken English, "Thank you."

When word got out that I was interested, Tommy Mottola, who was running Sony Music Entertainment at the time—no surprise to me—moved in and signed her to a deal, so I produced only part of her English-language debut album, *Unison*. I was amazed by what a pro she was. She was such a pro, in fact, that one day, while we were recording, I looked out of the studio window and noticed that the workmen had just finished resurfacing my tennis court, and were in fact in the process of taking down the tape. I had been waiting for that day for three months, and I was anxious to use the court, so I turned to Celine and said, "Honey, I just want to bounce a ball on my tennis court for a minute, just to get that feeling. I'll be right back." She nod-

My parents Maurice and Eleanor, wedding photo, 1940, Victoria, BC

Me age four, 1953

Me and my father

With Stan Getz, when I thought jazz was my future, back in 1962.

My "Beatles Band" at the age of fourteen. Bandmates from left: Neil Sinclair, Ken McCloud, John McCarther, me, and best friend Cris Earthy.

The band in 1966 in London, wearing outfits inspired by Paul Revere and the Raiders.

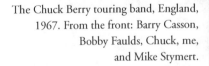

The Chuck Berry touring band, England, 1967. From the front: Barry Casson, Bobby Faulds, Chuck, me, and Mike Stymert.

(Above) Performing with
Skylark in 1973 with
my then-wife B.J. Cook,
who was expecting.

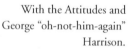

With the Attitudes and
George "oh-not-him-again"
Harrison.

In the studio with Earth,
Wind & Fire genius
Maurice White, 1979.

On the Merv Griffin Show. Merv loved music and the people that made it.

No better feeling than the power of an orchestra.

The Blended Family; clockwise from top left, Mom, Amy, Linda, Erin, Brody, Brandon, me, Jordan, Sara.

Sharing Producer of the Year honor with Lionel Ritchie at the 1984 Grammys.

Skating with The Oilers
(the hottest hockey team
of the 80s)—Kevin Lowe,
me, Wayne Gretzky,
and Fee Waybill
(of The Tubes).

With Alan Thicke,
Rob Lowe, and
Wayne Gretzky on
our way to
the first David Foster
Foundation gala
in 1986.

With one of our foundation kids, Jamie Cormier and his sister.

With Canadian prime minister Brian Mulroney and daughter Jordan at the Foster Foundation softball fundraiser, Victoria, BC, 1986.

Receiving the order of Canada in 1988
from the Governor General, who was representing the Queen.

Working on a Neil Diamond album in 1989 at my studio in Malibu.

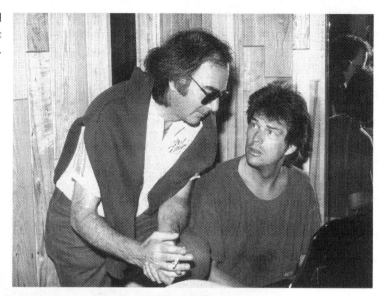

With Celine Dion in the studio, 1990.

Michael Jackson, Linda, and our kids.

With Whitney—the *Bodyguard* meets the Grammys.

With Terry Semel and Bob Daly, co-chairmen of Warner Bros. Pictures and Warners Music Group, with whom I've been working for more than a decade.

Recording with the BeeGees in 1997: Maurice, Me, Barry, and Robin.

Me and Kevin Sharp at the Bogart Gala.

With my mother, Eleanor, 1998.

With Kenny G and
Johnny Mathis at Craig and
Susan McCaw's wedding.

Rehearsing for the Agassi Gala
with Rod Stewart and
Elton John.

With President Clinton and my mother at Ronnie Hawkins's X-rated birthday party.

With Celine and Barbra, two of the greatest voices on the planet, at a 70s-themed party.

With Muhammad Ali at his annual "Fight Night" gala fundraiser, Phoenix, 2004.

Me with Paul Anka in 2004.

Working on Josh Groban's Christmas album at Abbey Road Studios in London, summer 2007, with Humberto Gatica, (left) and Josh (right).

Me and Yolanda in Holland, 2007.

Working out some details of Bocelli's TV special in his hometown in Italy, summer 2007.

Summer 2007 in Italy with two of my favorite musicians: trumpet whiz Chris Botti and classical pianist phenom Lang Lang.

Me and Yolanda, 2007.

With Quincy Jones in London, 2007.

With sisters Jeanie, Maureen, Ruth, Marylou, and Jaymes in Mexico, 2007.

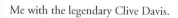

Me with the legendary Clive Davis.

Cooking with Wolfgang Puck and Bill Gates at Tim Blixseth's Yellowstone Club.

On stage with Michael Bublé.

With Hillary Clinton, 2007.

My daughters. Clockwise from top left: Amy, Erin, Jordan, and Sara.

Jordan's big college grad day; left to right, Sara, proud Dad, Jordan, Erin.

2008: My five beautiful daughters; left to right, Sara, Allison, Erin, Amy, Jordan.

Surrounded by some of my very talented friends at the finale of my PBS special.

With Alice and Cheryl Cooper at the Muhammad Ali event,
Phoenix, 2008.

ded and smiled, but with her limited English I'm not sure she understood a word I'd said.

Humberto and I went outside and we started hitting balls to each other, and before we knew it we were playing an entire set. And I looked up and saw Celine standing at the microphone, watching us, hardly moving, and I felt awful. And forty-five minutes later, when we walked back into the studio, both of us drenched in sweat, she was still standing there, at the microphone—and she *smiled* at me. Unbelievable.

After seeing what Celine could do in the studio, I was even crazier about her. I went around telling everyone in the world about Celine, saying she was going to be the Next Big Thing. I introduced her to people. I put her in front of charity crowds. I arranged meetings with other artists. I remember telling Kenny Loggins about her—we were working on something together—and I had to beg him to give her a chance to record with him. "I never heard of her," he said. "French-Canadian? Does she even speak English?"

"Please, Kenny, just try her."

So she returned to my studio in Malibu, and the moment she opened her mouth it was as if time had stopped again. Kenny couldn't even sing. He was paralyzed. She was *that* good. It took him a couple of minutes to recover. "Holy shit!" he said.

A few months later I took part in a corporate gig for the Holiday Inn, in Atlanta, organized by my good friend Michael Marto and his company, Executive Visions, and the other Kenny—Kenny Rogers—was part of the featured entertainment. He wanted to do a duet with Sheena Easton—we had produced "We've Got Tonight" together—but she wasn't available, so I suggested Celine. "She's the perfect girl for this," I said. "She is going to blow your mind."

"I don't know, David . . ."

He was just as bad: different Kenny, same response. But I convinced him to give her a chance.

Celine flew in the next day and I introduced her to Kenny at the hotel bar. People saw us and began freaking out. "My God! Isn't that Kenny Rogers?!"

There was a guy playing piano at the bar, and I didn't have much time to show Kenny what Celine could do, so I went over and asked him if I could take over for a few minutes. As soon as he stepped aside, we launched in. Kenny sang the first four lines, with Celine looking at him adoringly, and then she opened her mouth—*Who needs tomorrow* . . . —and Kenny's face just dropped. Like, *Jesus! Who is this girl?*

It was a great moment for me—I'd been right, the plan worked—but the sad truth is that I was still struggling professionally (by my standards, anyway). When Celine's album came out, there was one hit on it, "Where Does My Heart Beat Now," and it wasn't one of the songs I'd produced.

Then I got a call from Ottawa asking me if I was willing to fly up and put a show together for a tribute to Prince Charles and Princess Diana, and of course—as a proud Canadian—I said yes. I enlisted Celine as the featured performer, and it went beautifully, and at the dinner afterward I was seated right next to Diana. Prime Minister Brian Mulroney, a very likable guy who I was meeting for the first time, was on her other side. As dinner got underway, I remember thinking how grateful I was to Paul Anka, who had taken the time to show me which fork to use.

At one point during the meal Diana asked me to tell her some dumb-blonde jokes, and the prime minister said, "No, no, you can't do that! That's not appropriate!" But she insisted, so I told her a couple of wild stories, including one about a blonde who always ended up with her underpants around her ankles. Diana laughed at all the right places. She was very charming and seductive. "You know," she told me at one point, resting her bejeweled hand on my arm and batting her eyes, "Fergie has the reputation for being the bad one in the family, but she's not. *I'm* the bad one."

Linda, meanwhile, was at another table, sitting next to Charles, with the actor Michael J. Fox directly across from them. And she understood the protocol better than I did, because apparently you're not supposed to speak to them unless they address you first. That wasn't a problem for Linda, however, because Charles was very friendly, and he kept gabbing away, but he never said a word to Michael J. Fox, who seemed to be getting increasingly frustrated, and who refrained from addressing Prince Charles because he, too, had been coached on proper protocol. Finally, he couldn't take it anymore. "Linda," he said loudly. "Why don't you say 'Hello' or 'What do you think, Michael?' or ask me how I'm doing so I can get in on this conversation?"

It was a terrific evening. I as usual did the music, and I also put together a romantic little montage of film clips and photographs and interviews to go with one of the songs, focusing of course on Charles and Diana. And when it was over, the prime minister took me aside and said, "I don't know if you were aware of this, but Charles and Diana are on a downward slide, and that little presentation of yours—I could see how much it moved them both. It almost brought Diana to tears."

I had no idea that their marriage was in trouble. Then again, they had no idea that *my* marriage was in trouble.

When we got back to L.A. I was still facing the same old problems, both personally—and more worrisome—professionally. I began to wonder whether I was finished, and that's when I heard from Natalie Cole's people. She was trying for a comeback, and all I could think was, *Join the club.*

6

Barbra. Madonna. Michael.

After the unexpected success of *Unforgettable: With Love,* and after that amazing experience on *The Bodyguard,* my life literally came crashing to a halt when, late one night, I plowed into Ben Vereen with my Chevy Suburban. Eventually, I was able to speak with Ben on the phone—"Good hit"—and two weeks later, when he was up and about, I finally got permission from the hospital to visit him. Considering that I thought I'd killed him, he looked great. "You know," I said, "other than the day my father died, that day on PCH was the worst day of my life."

"It wasn't my best day, either," he said, smiling. "But I'm feeling much better."

He went on to make a full recovery.

Three months later, I was tooling along the PCH again, in the middle of the day, not a hundred yards from the scene of my earlier accident, when I heard a roar and looked up to see part of the mountain crumbling just ahead of me. Being more than mildly claustrophobic, and thinking I was going to be buried alive, I hit the gas, hoping to outrun the landslide, and I struck that wall of earth—600 tons of dirt and rock—at eighty miles an hour. Except for the driver's seat, the car was totaled.

If anybody had been in the car with me, they would have been killed.

I remember thinking, *I am the luckiest guy in the world.*

Several weeks after that harrowing second accident, I found myself, once again, producing for my old friend and Malibu neighbor, Barbra Streisand. I love Barbra, and I've actually grown to love her exacting standards. Everyone thinks she's a perfectionist, and she may well be, but putting that label on her really misses the point.

There are two principal things you need to know about Barbra. The first is that she likes people to get things right. If she's reading a lyric sheet, for example, and they've got the wrong word in there—"and" instead of "but"—you will be corrected. She doesn't like spelling errors and dropped letters, either. I used to think, *Just chill, Barbra. Take your pencil and put an F in front of the O and the R, and there's your word, F-O-R.* But as I get older, I see her point. If you're going to do a job, any job, why can't you do it right? If I hire you to do something, why should I have to come up behind you sweeping up the mess you made? Just do it right. Period. I don't think that's too much to ask, and neither, obviously, does Barbra. She hates incompetence, and she taught me to hate it, too.

The second thing—and this is what earned Barbra her reputation—is far more significant, and simply put it's this: Barbra needs to know every single option that's available to her, which I don't think is exactly the same as being a perfectionist. Could the note go this way? Could the note go that way? Could that chord go here? Could that chord go there? Could it go slower? Could it go faster? Could we use this note as the intro instead of that one? Could we wait a bit longer before we introduce the horns?

And it's tough, of course. That's *my* job. Some of these seemingly random, tiny changes often mean that the entire orchestra has to go back to the beginning to redo a single bar. But that's Barbra. That's her process. She's also a brilliant film director, and if she were shooting a scene with twelve helicopters, and one of them came in at the slightly wrong angle, Barbra would probably want to re-shoot the entire scene. It might be only half a minute of footage in the finished film, but she's going to get it right. So, yeah, I guess she is a perfectionist, but she's a *perfectionist with purpose,* and in my book that makes it okay. That's why I can work with her—most of the time, anyway—because I know what to expect.

And here's the thing: When you're making a record, not every little fix is going to make a difference in the final product. How many people are going to be able to say, "That note was out of tune"? But if you don't approach the work by trying to make your record as perfect as possible, it's never going to be as good as it can be. *Don't be sloppy.* About any of it. It might seem like minutiae, but it matters.

Would it really kill the Rolling Stones to tune their guitars once in a while? And Neil Young: I remember busting him once for singing out of tune, and he shot back, "Hey, man! That's my *sound.*"

That isn't to say that working with Barbra is always a barrel of laughs. Sometimes she tries to produce herself. She'll say, "Let's go to the next track." And I have to say, "No, Barbra. Let's finish this track first."

Or she'll say, "I have an idea. I want to try something."

"Barbra," I'll say. "We're mixing."

And she'll say, "This will only take thirty seconds."

And of course three hours later you're still working on that thirty-second fix, because she's a visionary—she sees and hears things others miss, and she needs to address them.

Now that I think back on it, though, we did have one memorable disagreement during the making of her *Back to Broadway* album. There was a technical glitch at one point—something on the board malfunctioned—and she turned to me and snapped. "You're an amateur!"

"Me?" I said. "You're the one that's difficult to work with!"

"Me? I'm not difficult. *You're* difficult!"

"Really?" I shot back. "If we're both so difficult, why are we working together?"

And she went all *Funny Girl* on me, with the hand gestures and everything, and said, "Because nobody else will work with us?"

And both of us broke down laughing.

Another time we were at one of my old studios, which I'd thrown together in the garage of Linda's house (you can make records anywhere) and the chairs were pretty ratty. (I work; I don't decorate.) During a pause in the session, Barbra looked over at my chairs as if she wanted to burn them. "Those chairs are filthy and disgusting!" she said.

"If you don't like them, why don't you get me some new ones!" I said.

And the next day two new chairs arrived.

That's Barbra.

The thing is, if I had to get bailed out of jail, I'd feel comfortable calling her at four in the morning. She'd probably say, "Do you have any idea what time it is?" But twenty minutes later she'd be at the precinct to save my ass.

And she's always been there for me. Once, while we were working on her *Back to Broadway* album, the herniated disc in my back got so bad that Linda had to drive me to the hospital. Since I don't take elevators, I had to crawl up nine flights of stairs to the room I'd been assigned, and I ended up staying for five days.

On the third day, Barbra was talking to Linda, to see how I was getting on. Linda said she was on her way to the hospital, with her two boys, Brandon and Brody, and Barbra offered to meet her there and take the boys to the movies, which would be a lot more entertaining than visiting their stepfather in the hospital.

Before any of them had arrived, a large nurse came into the room to give me another shot of Demerol. I was on my stomach, with my ass exposed, and the nurse had the syringe in her hand. She had just given it a little tap and squirt, to get rid of the air bubble, when Barbra walked into the room.

And both of them screamed at the same time: "Oh my God!"

The nurse screamed because she couldn't believe that Barbra Streisand had just walked into the room. And Barbra probably screamed because she didn't like the looks of my ass.

A few minutes later, Linda and the boys showed up, and Barbra, fully recovered at this point, took the boys to the movies.

Within a few days, Barbra and I were back at work. We were putting the finishing touches on "Some Enchanted Evening," one of my favorite tracks on that album, and we were butting heads a bit—two perfectionists trying to get everything perfectly right. I didn't think either of us was being more difficult than usual, but years later I was out to dinner with some mutual friends who had been there to watch part of the session, and the wife was talking about how heated things became. "Don't tell me you don't remember, David! You almost brought Barbra to tears that night."

"I did?" I said. This was a revelation to me.

"Yes! You were incredibly mean to her."

"I was? What was I doing?"

"You kept pushing her to do the vocals your way and she found it very upsetting. You were at the piano doing this swirly bit and you kept telling her that she needed to go higher."

"I don't remember that at all!" I protested.

"Well if you ever write a book about your life," she said, "you better put that in there."

Maybe I am an asshole sometimes. It's certainly possible. In my quest for perfection, I can be tough. But I've been surrounded by toughness my whole life. I had a strong mother. I have six sisters. I have four daughters and a fifth daughter I learned about only a few years ago (I'll get to that story in due course.) I've had three wives. And I've worked with some very powerful women in my day, including Barbra Streisand. I guess you could say I've spent my life immersed in estrogen, so I can handle it. And you know, there are worse things in life.

Around that same time, toward the end of his tenure as prime minister, Brian Mulroney called to say he was going to be the featured speaker at the Ronald W. Reagan Presidential Library, and that he and his wife, Mila, would like to follow that up by coming to visit us in Los Angeles. I spoke to Linda about it and we decided to put a big party together for them at Splash, a Malibu restaurant owned by my good friend Richard Chesterfield. We had to clear it with the government, and on the appointed day Brian and Mila showed up in one of ten black Suburbans, protected by a small army of cops in full riot-gear. They had pat-downs at the restaurant entrance, bomb-sniffing dogs, and snipers on the surrounding rooftops.

It was kind of cool.

It was also a great party. We had Lionel Richie, Merv Griffin, Dick Clark, Ed McMahon, Natalie Cole, and of course Streisand, because Mulroney had told me he was a huge fan, and because she's a political junkie. Everybody sang and performed, and I accompanied them on piano. Natalie Cole did "Unforgettable." Lionel Richie did "Truly." And the prime minister did "When Irish Eyes Are Smiling," and he wasn't half-bad. When he was done, an astonishing thing happened. Barbra Streisand got to her feet and said, "If Prime Minister Mulroney can get up and sing at a private party, by God, so can I!" And she came over and stood next to me at the piano and sang "Some Enchanted Evening." She was phenomenal, as always.

After the performance, Ed McMahon came up to me, shaking his head in disbelief. "You know something," he said. "I've lived in this town for thirty years, and I've been to a lot of parties, and Barbra has been to a lot of the same parties, and this was the first time I've seen her do anything like that."

I think he was right. Up until that day, I had never heard Barbra sing at a private party, and I seriously doubt I'll ever hear her do it again. And it's funny, because I remember telling her once, "Barbra, if I had a voice like you I'd walk up to complete strangers on the street and say, 'Hey! Wanna see what I can do?' And then I'd bust out in song."

The prime minister kept telling me what a great time he'd had, and it made me feel good. I love him, and I love his wife, Mila. Great family, great kids—Canada's version of the Kennedys (without the drama). And you know, now that I think about it, some three or four years later, long after Mulroney left office, he came to L.A. again, and I went to pick him up at the Ritz-Carlton in Marina del Rey. He was standing outside, alone, waiting for me, and I found that truly amazing. He had gone from a high-level security detail to a visiting tourist in a matter of years. "Does it bother you?" I asked him.

"Absolutely not," he said. "I love being a regular citizen again. I love normal life."

I had expected to hear him say that he missed the power and the attention, but he seemed genuinely happy.

As for my own life, things had taken a rather shocking turn. I'd been in a brief slump some years earlier, but in 1993 I woke up to seven Grammy nominations. I didn't win any of them, unfortunately, but *Billboard* singled me out as Top Singles Producer and Top R&B Producer of the year.

That winter, Interscope Records released *David Foster: The Christmas Album.* It featured Natalie Cole, Celine Dion, Michael Crawford, Tom Jones, Johnny Mathis, Vanessa Williams, BeBe and CeCe Winans, Tammy Wynette, Wynonna, and Peabo Bryson and Roberta Flack. It did so well that it was subsequently turned into an NBC television special.

My professional life was in high gear. I had my groove back.

The biggest, richest check I ever got—up to that point, anyway—was my first royalty check from *The Bodyguard:* It was for $1,000,000. I loved holding that check so much that for days on end I refused to deposit it. I kept it between the two front seats of my Chevy Suburban—the Vereen Machine, as Ben called it—and every time I came to a red light I would pick it up and look at it again. One million dollars! I couldn't believe it.

One night I drove to Venice to showcase *Scream,* the musical I'd been working on with my friend Art Janov, and found myself in a funky section of town. When the show was over I returned to my truck and noticed that the passenger side window had been shattered. I drew closer. The stereo system had been ripped out, and a few personal effects were gone, and suddenly I remembered the check.

I looked between the seats and there it was, a million bucks. Thank God for stupid criminals.

The next morning, early, I went to the bank and deposited it.

The teller smiled *very* warmly.

Shortly thereafter, I took that money and put it toward a stunning 22-acre compound in Malibu. I called it my *Bodyguard* house. The previous house, also in Malibu but far more modest, was my *Chicago* house, and my starter house, the one in Toluca Lake, was my *Earth, Wind & Fire* house.

The Malibu compound was in a class by itself, however. It had taken me a quarter of a century to get there, but I was finally living large. Now, I must tell you, I enjoyed living large, but I will never do it again. In very short order, my personal life was like an industry. We had sixteen manicured acres, a tennis court, a guardhouse, three guesthouses, two recording studios, 14,000 square feet of living space, *nineteen* bathrooms—it was ridiculous. It took a small army to run the place. As my friend Cher once told me (borrowing a line that's been attributed to everyone from Mae West to Sophie Tucker): "I've been poor, and I've been rich—and rich is better." But it does get a little out of hand.

Not long after that purchase, as luck would have it, I got a call from Atlantic Records. They wanted to recruit me as a vice president, and I took the job without giving it a second thought. It wasn't a full-time job, and I wasn't exclusive to the label, so I still had my freedom, and the offer had come at a very good time—I had a mortgage to pay on that stunning ocean-view spread. I'm not saying I was worried about money, but I can tell you from personal experience that people are never quite as rich as you think they are. Bill Gates has money, certainly, but if he started cashing out his stock, Microsoft would collapse before he got to his third billion—making the rest of it worthless.

Atlantic was a Warner Music Group label, and the guy who offered me the job was Doug Morris, who was running the place at the time. I had met him in the mid-1980s, when I was doing *St. Elmo's Fire,* and he had signed me as an artist through a deal orchestrated by Ned Shankman, my then-manager. I did three solo albums for Atlantic, made something of a name for myself (especially in Asia), and now—a decade later—I was back as an executive.

I love Doug—he is currently chairman of Universal Music and, I think he is one of the greatest executives in the business—and I'll always remember something he said to me when I was working on "Tap Dance" for the movie *White Nights.* I was flying high, and I expected the song to be as successful as the love theme from *St. Elmo's,* but Doug didn't agree. "It ain't a hit, man," he said. "Why is it you guys always think everything you do is a hit?" I didn't say this then because I hadn't thought of it, but the answer is really quite simple: We need self-delusion to propel us forward. If I didn't truly believe it was going to be a hit, why the hell was I writing it?

The other part of it is that we tend to believe our own press, especially if it's good. It's easy to write off the bad reviews as the work of morons who know absolutely nothing about music, and you almost have to do that to survive. But there's another side to it, and I often point that out to young artists: "If you don't believe the good press, you won't have to believe the bad press." Unfortunately, I am seldom able to take my own advice.

One of the first things I did in my new capacity as a V.P. at Atlantic was to sign the Corrs. I'd heard about them from Jason Flom, a very talented A&R guy at Atlantic with a label of his own. "Man," he told me, "I just saw this group. They're really great, but it's not my type of music." The group was comprised of three sisters and a brother who did Irish-pop fusion, and the two albums I produced, *Forgiven Not Forgotten* and *Talk on Corners,* sold twenty million units in Europe alone.

I also worked with All-4-One. At Doug Morris's urging, I took John Michael Montgomery's country smash "I Swear" and turned it into a smooth R&B number that became a crossover hit and stayed at the top of the pop charts for eleven weeks. (This was similar to what I had done with "I Will Always Love You," re-imagining a great country song in an entirely different genre.) For eleven weeks, Doug and I would get the *Billboard* charts every Tuesday morning, before they hit the streets, and both of us would quickly check to see if "I Swear" was still at the top spot. Then we'd call each other: "Yup. Still there." On the twelfth week, when the song finally dropped, we didn't even talk. In fact, I don't think we talked for the rest of the week.

The other thing that happened during this period is that I began laying the foundations for a record company of my own, and I went to my friend and manager, Brian Avnet, whom I'd known since my *Rocky Horror* days, and asked him if he was interested in running the company. When he signed on, I approached Atlantic about making it a joint venture, and the result was 143 Records. (The name means "I love you": one letter, four letters, three letters.)

One of the very first guys we signed to the label was Kevin Sharp, whom I had met a couple of years earlier through the Make-A-Wish Foundation. Kevin had a rare form of Ewing's sarcoma, a virulent and usually deadly bone cancer, and he had been given little chance of recovery. For some reason, he told the foundation that he wanted to meet me. On the appointed day, he showed up at my studio with his father, Glen, and what was supposed to be a two-hour visit turned into a very full day, Kevin and his father ended up spending the night. During the visit, Kevin told me that he wanted to be a singer, and we went into the recording studio and gave it a shot, but he was so weak that he was barely audible. The next morning, before he left, I told him to come back when he felt stronger, and to never give up on his dream. Though honestly, from the looks of him—thin and frail and bald from the chemotherapy—I didn't believe he was long for the world.

Two years later, my sister Jaymes came across an unsolicited submission, and she remembered his name, and we listened to the recordings and were completely blown away. The tape had been sitting in a box for many months, and I imagined that Kevin was no longer alive, when in fact the cancer had gone into remission. Long story short: We brought him into the studio, hooked him up with a country division of Atlantic, and before we knew it he had four Top 10 hits, including

"Nobody Knows," which stayed at Number One for four weeks. A million CDs later, he was a star. And all I could think was, *Holy shit! The power of music!* Kevin's desire to fulfill a dream, coupled with a little friendly encouragement, had changed his life.

To this day, whenever I see Kevin's father he immediately starts crying.

Throughout this period, I worked with everybody from Madonna and Michael Jackson to Leann Rimes and R&B wizard Kenneth "Babyface" Edmonds.

When Madonna first called, I was a little surprised—my music isn't really hip enough for her—but I guess her camp thought we should meet, and I got a call from Liz Rosenberg, the PR maven who has been with Madonna from the beginning. I knew Liz from my early days at Warners, and I trust her because she is truly the best of the best. "David, how would you like to have dinner with Madonna?" she said.

"I think I could manage that," I said.

Two weeks later, I was sitting in a Manhattan restaurant, across from Madonna, and I found her so seductive that she left me almost spellbound.

"Have you seen *Truth or Dare?*" she asked at one point, referring to her 1991 film.

"No, I'm sorry," I admitted. "I haven't."

"You should watch it," she said.

I didn't take that as a suggestion. I took it as a direct order.

Before I'd had a chance to watch the film, however, she decided she liked me enough to work with me, and not long after we met at my Malibu studio for our first session. It was ten in the morning and she showed up in nylons, a short skirt, high heels, and a see-through top—the full Madonna package. It was wild.

She had an amazing work ethic, though. She was on time every day and was really co-producing the songs with me. A lot of artists want to produce just because they can, and they don't do a thing for the credit, which I really hate. But Madonna worked as hard as any producer I know.

In the middle of our sessions, feeling somewhat smitten, I actually took the time to watch *Truth or Dare*. I enjoyed the movie, but I had trouble with a couple of parts. The scene with my friend Kevin Costner, for example, bothered me a little. In the film, he went backstage after one of her concerts to tell Madonna how much he had enjoyed it, and he made the mistake of describing the performance as "neat." After he left, Madonna pretended to stick her finger down her throat and said, "Anybody who says my show is 'neat' has to go."

When she asked me what I thought of the film, I told her I thought it was good—"really interesting." I didn't mention the Costner bit, but I said that the scene where two guys kissed kind of turned me off. I don't think I'm homophobic, but that scene felt wrong on all sorts of levels. Madonna didn't appreciate my response. "If that bothered you, you're too square for me," she said.

"Just being honest," I said.

"I'm fighting for stuff like that," she went on. "I want two guys kissing to be normal. You're too square for me when you think the way you think." She was really annoyed, and she couldn't help herself: "You represent everything I'm trying to change."

Minutes later, however, we were back at work. On some level it would have been nice if Madonna thought I was the coolest guy she'd ever met, but it didn't really matter, and she certainly didn't let her opinion of me affect the work.

At the end of the day, the songs we did together were not particularly impressive, though one of them, "You'll See," was *really neat*. Madonna had written a great lyric (*You think that I can't live without your love / You'll see*) and I thought my music was great, and the song actually became a Top 5 hit, but it didn't drive the album. It was a Greatest Hits album—*Something to Remember*, released by Maverick Records—

and you always put two or three new songs on these albums in the hopes of getting a breakout single that will propel sales, but that didn't happen for us. It was not our greatest moment; not hers, and not mine. But I liked the whole experience of working with her—the punctuality, the professionalism, and the sexiness.

Strangely enough, we worked together again not long after—so how square could I be, really? "You'll See" had become a hit, and she wanted to do it in Spanish, and she decided to record the vocal in Miami, in Gloria and Emilio Estefan's studio. She called and said, "You've got to stay in the Delano Hotel in South Beach. You'll love it."

So I flew down and checked into the Delano and I couldn't believe it. The fucking hotel had cement floors and cement walls and the bed was on the floor. I like my bed to be raised up a little, so that I don't have to push off first thing in the morning just to get on my feet. This hotel was her style, not mine, and I was definitely too square for the place.

I didn't complain, though. I showed up at the studio and Emilio was there, hanging out with Madonna, and before long we got to work. At one point, however, with no warning whatsoever, Madonna suddenly stopped singing. I looked into the booth and I couldn't see her, so I crossed the room and went inside. She was flat on her back on the floor in some kind of Zen pose, and she looked very sad.

"What's wrong?" I said.

"I don't know," she said.

"You feeling okay?"

"I just need a man," she said. "I need to be with a real man."

And the thing is, there was nothing sexual about it. The comment spoke to her vulnerability and loneliness, and I found it very touching, and in fact it made me like her more than ever. A few minutes later, with a deep, heartfelt sigh, she got to her feet and continued, and for the rest of the session she was the *tough* Madonna, not the vulnerable Madonna who was looking for a soulmate.

The other megastar I worked with during this period was Michael Jackson, producing several tracks for the *HIStory* album. We were recording at the Hit Factory in Manhattan, and I remember coming back to the studio after lunch one day to find a twenty-foot python slithering across the console. I didn't go anywhere near the console, of course, and Michael showed up a moment later, picked up the snake, and took it away.

Michael is probably one of the most complex guys on the planet, but he was okay to work with. He actually *worked*. He was always engaged and focused, and my biggest complaint is that he had a tendency to do dozens of takes of every song. I can't think past eight takes, so it made me crazy. I'm not one of those genius chess masters who are always thinking seventeen moves ahead, so I found that part of it more than a little frustrating. And I don't think a good singer needs more than eight takes to get it right. There's a law of diminishing returns, and I think even the best singers reach it after six or seven takes.

If you think about it, though, Michael had his finest hour when he was working with Quincy Jones. Now *that* was definitely lightning in a bottle. Those two caught a moment in time, never to be repeated. The rest of us, all the other producers who tried to work with him subsequently, could never even hope to come close to that. We were just dicking around, frankly.

Michael was also interesting to hang out with. The better I got to know him, the more elusive he seemed. One moment, in a little-boy voice, he would curse the head of Sony Music. "That Tommy Mottola is a mean person," he'd say, sounding like a six-year-old. In the studio he'd be a pro, almost a regular guy, and we really connected. (He struck me as Frank Sinatra and Gene Kelly rolled into one.) And with Lisa Marie Presley, whom he was dating at the time, he would be someone else entirely.

Interestingly enough, my then-wife Linda had once dated Elvis, so she and Lisa Marie actually knew each other fairly well. You might say that for a brief period Linda had played the role of Lisa's stepmom.

Anyway, the kids were visiting from Los Angeles—three of my daughters and Linda's two sons—and one night they decided they wanted to go to the movies. We were staying at the Plaza Hotel, and Michael had rented me a magnificent suite—on a low floor—that must have had six bedrooms. It was a palace, a lot better than that Zen-like concrete bunker at the Delano.

"I can't go to the movies," Michael said. They knew what he meant: He couldn't go out in public without creating a shit-storm among the paparazzi.

And one of the kids said, "We can dress you up and disguise you."

And that's what they did. They got in the elevator and went up to his suite and dressed him up in their own clothes. They put a scarf on him, and some jeans, and they tucked his hair under a cap and turned it to one side, gangster-style. Michael wasn't wild about hiding the curl, though; he wanted it right out there on his forehead, for the whole world to see. The kids told him he had to hide the curl because it was a dead giveaway, but he was adamant. "No, no. I've got to have my curl out," he said. I thought that was very telling. He didn't want to be seen, but he *kind of* wanted to be seen—which I guess is often the issue if you're famous.

Then they argued about what movie to see. My kids voted for *Speed;* Michael was more interested in *Little Big League.* Hmm.

We had the valet bring the van around, and we piled in without incident. There were some paparazzi out front, but they must have looked at us and figured we were nobodies. And it was very interesting, because Michael and Lisa got separated when everyone scrambled into the van, and it was clear that he wanted her to sit next to him. On the way to the movie theater, he turned to her and said, "Lisa, here. Come here. Sit here." He said it just like a regular man, not in that little-boy voice of his. It was like, *You're going to sit with me, woman,* and she did. I was very impressed, but I was also confused. I mean, *Who was this guy?*

Maybe she brought the testosterone out in him. I don't know. But I know this: She loved him. And that relationship became one of the biggest tabloid nightmares of all time.

I actually ended up working with Lisa Marie a decade later, long after the romance with Michael ended. One of the tracks was a duet— Lisa Marie and her father, Elvis—not unlike the duet I'd done with Natalie Cole and *her* father, mixing the old with the new. The song was called "Daddy Don't Cry," and Lisa got very emotional when I first played back the mix. The song was really a commemoration of her father's death, some thirty years earlier, and—having lost my own father—I knew how much that had to hurt. I still think about my father every day. He instilled a solid sense of morals and goodness in all his children, and his greatness stays with me in everything I do.

Lisa ended up not releasing that song because she didn't want to use her father's fame to launch her own career. But she told me that working with me had given her the confidence to become a recording artist, and of course I enjoyed hearing that.

During this same period, Whitney Houston wanted to know if I'd be available to work with her on a couple of tracks for *The Preacher's Wife,* and she asked me to leave my comfort zone and fly to New York. I'd done it for Michael Jackson, and I did it again for Whitney.

When I got to her house, where she had a studio, I waited for six hours. I am a bit of a stickler about punctuality—if someone keeps me waiting, they are basically telling me that their time is more important than mine—so you can imagine how difficult this was for me. Eventually, I left and went back to the hotel.

I returned the next day and she kept me waiting for another six hours, and finally she sent a note: "I'm sorry. You understand. You're married. You've got kids. You know what it's like. I'm dealing with a bunch of stuff right now, and I can't sing. I'm really very sorry." I did understand, because I could relate to family drama, but I didn't like having my time wasted.

I had dinner that night with Clive Davis, who had arranged this whole thing, just as he'd done with *The Bodyguard* soundtrack, and I was still a little irked. "I want you to pass on a message to Whitney," I said. "Tell her that next time she wants to sing with me, it'll be at my studio, at my house in Malibu. That way, if she's late, at least I'll be in the comfort of my own environment."

Clive, the consummate diplomat, has been known to ruffle more than his fair share of feathers, but at the end of the day he has a gift for making everybody happy. Several weeks later Whitney flew out to work with me and we had three glorious days together. On the second day, though, while I was in the studio, I heard Whitney and Bobby in the room next door, whooping it up big-time. I went off to investigate and found them in front of the TV, watching my DVD of Jerry Springer's most outrageous outtakes, and clearly loving the show. I am a big fan of Jerry Springer myself. I was also a big fan of Bob Barker and of *The Price is Right*. I wish CBS had picked me to host the new version of that show, not Drew Carey. (Note to Les Moonves: I am still available. And I'm not kidding. I love game shows. And I'm not kidding about that, either.)

Just before I wrapped with Whitney, Clive called to see how we were getting along. I told him she was a perfect angel, and I thanked him for arranging it. I honestly don't know how Clive does what he does, because I tend to piss people off left and right. He's not a guy who is necessarily useful in the recording process, but he has a real gift for finding great songs and for spotting talent, and—just as important—for making talent happy. Clive is a genuine star-maker.

When people ask me about Clive, I always tell them: "He makes stars. I make hits."

The following year I worked on *Secrets,* with Toni Braxton, and again with Celine Dion on *Falling Into You,* which must have had ten producers on it. I spent a lot of time in the top spot in the weeks and months ahead: "Unbreak My Heart," "I Will Always Love You," and "I Swear" spent *months* at Number One, and several others hovered in the Top 5.

With work consuming so much of my time, I really couldn't focus on the problems at home, with Linda, with my ex, and with my daughters. When I look back on it, I wonder if that isn't the Big Secret of Life: *Stay busy. Don't think. Everything will be fine.*

And you know something? For a time, everything *was* fine.

7

"Pop" as in "Popular"

Despite our problems, Linda and I had a very exciting social life. We became increasingly close friends with Barbara and Marvin Davis, who were as charming as they were wealthy. Marvin made a fortune as chairman of Davis Petroleum, and in the course of his long and very productive life owned everything from the Denver Broncos to the Beverly Hills Hotel to 20th Century Fox.

They had the best Hollywood parties I'd ever been to, and I must have been to dozens of them over the course of a decade. They lived in Beverly Hills, in a 25,000-square-foot house that included two guesthouses and a thirty-seat movie theater and was known, affectionately, as The Knoll. Barbara was the consummate wife and the perfect hostess, and she brought a level of party-giving to Los Angeles that hadn't been seen since the forties and has not been matched since. It was like

Europe in the days of the great salons. Everyone got dressed up, and every detail was elegant and impeccable. And no expense was spared. Imagine going to a Christmas party at someone's home and finding the Rockettes performing in the living room.

Rumor had it that people would leave town if they weren't invited so they could use that to explain their absence. "A party? Really? I was skiing in Aspen."

In addition to my doing the music for most of their fundraisers, they asked me to do the music for the party for their fiftieth wedding anniversary. I had Stevie Wonder there, and Kenny G, and Don Rickles did a beautiful job of insulting absolutely everyone. Larry King ended up turning the evening into a private TV special.

I met amazing people at the Davises'. Bill Clinton. Dustin Hoffman. Sidney Poitier. Joan Collins. Michael Caine. Tom Hanks. I was usually one of the few non-famous guests. And it's funny because one night I met a guy there called Barry Krost, who was then managing Jackie Collins, the mega-selling author and coolest chick in town. He told me that he used to work with Cat Stevens, and I immediately interrupted him to tell him my Cat Stevens story—the night he showed up at my dumpy little flat in London, wearing a crushed-velvet suit that matched his burgundy Rolls-Royce. "You're not going to believe this," Barry said. "I was the guy waiting in the Rolls-Royce."

The parties at the Davises' were really Hollywood at their finest, a bygone era. And at the end of the evening we'd invariably end up around the piano, with me playing. That's where a lot of those people discovered who I was, and how they ended up making me part of their lives, both personally and professionally. It's also how I ended up doing the Carousel of Hope Ball for Barbara, raising money for diabetes—which I continue to work on to this day—and how I became involved with the Race to Erase MS, with Barbara's daughter, Nancy. That first one for Nancy, we did in Aspen—and we got Kenny G, Michael

Bolton, and MC Hammer. They had a rockin', cowboy-themed party at the Little Nell, mixed in with ski races during the day.

But the best parties were the ones at The Knoll, back in L.A., and one year I actually ran into Frank Sinatra there. I went over to say hello, almost sure he'd remember me, because I'd produced one of the tracks on his 1993 *Duets* album, "I've Got a Crush on You," which we did with Barbra Streisand. Most people don't realize this, but these duets are generally put together in the studio. Frank sang his part, Barbra sang hers, and it was up to my engineers and me to make it sound as if they were on stage together, making eyes at each other as they crooned away. Not that you'd want to work with both of them at the same time, mind you: Two big stars in one room is one star too many.

I'd also seen Sinatra, briefly, during my session years, and had been excited about the fact that I was going to be working with him. But he walked into the studio that day, took a look at the assembled orchestra—which included me on piano—then turned and walked out. "No," he said. "Not today."

Years later I actually got a call from Jilly Rizzo, his longtime friend and confidant. Frank was looking around for a producer and Jilly got my name from my friend Carole Bayer Sager, one of the greatest songwriters ever.

"Carole tells me you're the best producer around," Jilly said.

"That's very flattering," I said. "But you shouldn't believe her. She's one of my best friends."

"Where would we record?" Jilly asked.

"At my studio," I said.

"Sixteen-track, right?"

"No, we're using twenty-four now."

"Twenty-four, huh? Let me talk to the boss."

He called a few days later and said, very politely, that it wasn't going to work. "The boss wants to do it his way," he said.

Of course he did. He was Frank Sinatra. He did everything his way. He even sang a song about it.

That night at the Davises', when I ran into Sinatra, I thought back to how that particular duet had come about. I'd been running around one crazy afternoon and had bumped into my friend Jay Landers, a hugely successful and talented A&R guy who had done a lot of work with Barbra, and his eyes lit up when he saw me. "Oh my God, David!" he said. "I don't know why I didn't think of you in the first place." He proceeded to tell me that he had been approached by Charles Koppelman, chairman of Capitol Records at the time, about asking Barbra if she would do a duet with Sinatra. Koppelman had recently won a very hard-fought battle to sign Frank, and it was his idea to create a duets album, because a regular Who's Who of recording artists wanted to sing with him.

Landers really loved the idea, so he talked to Phil Ramone, who was producing most of the album, and together they reviewed the few songs that still hadn't been assigned to other artists. He liked "I've Got a Crush on You" and took the idea to Barbra, and she agreed to do it if he could find a producer who could come up with a duet arrangement that worked. (This was the issue with all of the songs on the album, since none of them had been conceived as duets.) Landers reached out to various producers, but nothing clicked, and he felt that the opportunity to bring these two legends together was quickly slipping through his hands.

"Okay," I said, having heard enough. "Why don't you come by my studio tonight?" I'd always liked Jay Landers, a real song guy. Plus you know me: I can never say no; I need *something* to fill up those Saturdays and Sundays.

The challenge with these duets, as I said, is to make them *sound* as if the artists are standing at adjacent mikes, and somehow I managed to come up with an arrangement that pleased both Landers and Barbra. I think it turned out very well. The whole album was spectacular, and in fact it was the best-selling album of Frank's career. I'm not saying it was his best album, but it was definitely his most popular.

And that night at the Davises', seeing Frank standing there, looking a little unapproachable, but feeling that in some small way I had contributed to the album's success, I was struck by a brilliant idea. I went over and reintroduced myself, which didn't seem to make much of an impression on him, and then I laid on the charm. "I don't know if you're aware of it, but Barbra's also here tonight," I said. "Wouldn't it be great if the two of you sang that duet for the guests?"

He gave me a look like he wanted to take me outside and shoot me. "Why the fuck would I want to do that?" he said, then he turned and walked away.

That reminds me of another story, going way back to my Skylark days. I walked into the Whisky A Go Go, a club on Sunset Boulevard, and saw David Crosby sitting at the bar. I couldn't believe it. I was a huge fan of Crosby, Stills, Nash & Young, and I walked over to tell him so. I did the usual fawning-fan number: "Oh my God! David Crosby. I can't tell you what a pleasure it is to meet you. I am such a huge fan, yada yada yada." And he looked at me and bellowed, "Fuck you!" and stormed out.

Years later, I saw him and his wife at a restaurant, and I'd met her socially once or twice, and she called me over by name and told her husband, "You and David should work together. He's an incredible producer." And Crosby flashed a big smile and said, "Yeah, that would be great!" At which point I said, "You know, I'm a huge fan, but I have to tell you a story that happened twenty years ago." And he abruptly raised both hands and stopped me. "Before you start your story, let me apologize right now," he said. "I have no idea what you're going to tell me, but I'm sure it can't be good—because for the better part of a decade I was a total asshole."

• • •

When Marvin Davis passed away, in 2004, the parties stopped, but the experiences will remain with me forever. Marvin's death really *was* the end of an era, and there are many people in Hollywood who I know would agree with that assessment. I remember I was in British Columbia at the time of his funeral, but I flew back, at the family's request, to arrange the music. It was an incredibly moving service. Marvin's children and grandchildren gave emotional tributes, and several Hollywood heavyweights also got up to speak, including Sydney Poitier and Mo Ostin, who was arguably one of the most powerful record executives in history—he signed everyone from Frank Sinatra to Jimi Hendrix.

Michael Bublé sang "I'll Be Seeing You," Nita Whitaker sang "Heaven Holds the One I Love" (which I had written with Linda), and Carole Bayer Sager sang "That's What Friends Are For," and invited Stevie Wonder to sing with her. For the finale, I had everyone sing "Goodnight, Irene." It was a sad day for us all.

Meanwhile, I kept working.

In 1997, Celine's *Falling Into You* won the Grammy for Album of the Year, an honor I shared with a slew of other producers, and I won for Best Instrumental Arrangement with Accompanying Vocals, for Natalie Cole's "When I Fall in Love," which I produced with Alan Broadbent.

There's another reason that particular Grammy night sticks in my mind. Just before the ceremony, I saw Sting, and I went over to say hello to him, assuming, erroneously, that he knew who I was. "You know, Sting," I said, "whenever any reporter asks me who I have yet to work with that I would love to work with, my answer is always you." He kind of looked at me funny and walked away, and at that moment it occurred to me that he didn't have a clue who I was—which I found absolutely crushing, by the way.

Amazingly enough, when I won the Grammy, Sting was the guy presenting—and he put it in my hands. So afterward, at the big party, I saw him again, and I walked over, beaming. "So I guess this means that maybe you and I will actually get a chance to work together, huh?"

And he looked at me again, like, *Who the hell are you?* And it was doubly crushing.

Not long after, however, thanks to my friend Chris Botti, the genius trumpet player, whom I love and admire, I was reintroduced to Sting, and I think I saw a *glimmer* of recognition that time, so I'm not giving up hope. He's still on my Top 5 list of people I want to work with.

That same year, 1997, I was promoted to senior vice president at my other job, with the Warner Music Group, and a few months later Celine and Barbra teamed up on "A Tribute to David Foster." I still remember Barbra's opening line: "I can't believe they got me out of the house to honor someone who isn't running for office."

Tributes are a bit strange in the sense that they are like a memorial to you before you're dead. I used to think, naïvely, that they were about me, and I would get very excited. *These people actually want to honor me!* I felt like Sally Field at the Academy Awards ("I can't deny the fact that you like me!") But the tribute is only marginally about the person being honored; it's really about his or her Rolodex. If you have a good Rolodex, there's a better-than-average chance someone will come along and honor you someday, because these tributes are a great way to raise money for charity. That particular tribute raised money for the Neil Bogart Foundation, a division of City of Hope, one the biggest charities in the music business.

I'm not complaining, but I thought I should put it into perspective. The moment I got the call about the tribute, I had to get on the phone and start dialing like crazy. I had to call everyone I knew, from my billionaire friends to the friends who would have to borrow money from me to buy a table. I called absolutely everyone for whom I'd ever produced music. I called one of my contacts up north and the Royal Canadian Mounted Police sent twenty guys to stand guard at the door to impress the guests. You get the idea. Fourteen hundred people turned out. We raised a lot of money, and everyone was happy. I was happy, too, probably happier than everyone else. I like being Charity Boy. As I said, it makes me feel good about myself. And I have absolutely no shame when it comes to raising money for worthy causes.

As soon as that was over, I immediately went back to work, and I like to think of this period, the late nineties, as my Italian Period. This is when I first met Andrea Bocelli, the Italian tenor, and when I became friendly with the late Luciano Pavarotti, whom people always describe as "larger than life" for good reason.

Bocelli was actually brought to my studio by Tony Renis, an Italian who is an accomplished singer-songwriter in his own right. He was a friend of Bocelli's and wanted him to sing with Michael Bolton, and I was working with Bolton at the time, so Tony was looking for an introduction. I went to Bolton and suggested it, and Bolton wasn't interested. Still, I was curious about Bocelli and one evening I sat down to listen to his hit album, *Time to Say Goodbye.* The moment I heard his voice, I flipped out. He was that good. He was *beyond* good. (That Celine moment again.)

At the time, I was doing the music for *Quest for Camelot,* an animated feature, with my friend Carole Bayer Sager, and we had been working on a song called "The Prayer." That song came about after Dan Carlin, our music supervisor on the project, listened to everything we had written for *Camelot,* and honed in on a twenty-second melodic strain. "That's the part you should develop into a song," he said, and it turned out to be brilliant advice.

"There are only two people on the planet that can do our song," I told Carole the moment she picked up the phone. "Celine Dion and Andrea Bocelli."

I met Bocelli shortly thereafter, and I found him to be a truly amazing person. Blind since the age of twelve, he may well be one of the greatest singers on the planet (right up there with Celine, Barbra, and Whitney). When I work with him, I feel like I'm collaborating with Mozart. Plus he's fun on so many other levels—a real Renaissance Man. He's cultured, smart, funny, irreverent, loves good wine and fine dining, and he can play a half dozen instruments (sax, guitar, flute, trumpet, piano, and drums). He has an incredibly broad knowledge of music and is the only person I know, other than maybe Wynton Marsalis—whom I don't know personally—who can truly walk in both the pop world and the classical world. As for his voice, it is not of this earth. As Celine once said, "If God had a voice, it would be the voice of Andrea Bocelli."

We did "The Prayer" with Celine, and it was everything I had hoped it would be—and then some. Bocelli wasn't always easy to work with, but I don't think he's deliberately difficult. Still, if I asked for an extra take he would react as if I were trying to annoy him, which wasn't the case at all; I was just trying to make a better record. Also, back then, it was very difficult for him to sing in English, and he found the process frustrating. On the other hand, he can't have found me too annoying because he later asked me to write three songs for him for his *Cieli di Toscana* album. And I always enjoy working with him. Unlike many musicians, who are so focused on music that they are one-dimensional, Bocelli is a man with a huge appetite for life. I will travel way out of my comfort zone—all the way to Europe—because he's such great company, as well as a musical genius.

During one of those trips to Italy he took me out on his yacht one afternoon and then windsurfed back to shore, *alone*. I still can't figure out how he did it. And one night, after an evening out, we parked on the gravel driveway and there were five cars between us and the front door to the house. "Watch this!" he said. He zig-zagged his way between the cars, not even touching them, and emerged on the far side, grinning. Must have been the sound of the gravel—some kind of sonar.

After we did "The Prayer," I went around raving about Bocelli, and the following year we met again, when I asked him to contribute to Celine's 1998 Christmas album, *These Are Special Times*.

I followed that up by working with Celine and Luciano Pavarotti on "I Hate You, I Love You." During the making of that duet, Pavarotti invited me to his Manhattan apartment for dinner. He knew I was afraid of elevators, but I told him it wouldn't be a problem, and I took the stairs all the way to the twentieth floor. Celine was there, of course, and so was Tony Renis, the Italian who had introduced me to Bocelli, along with Humberto Gatica, and we had a terrific pasta dinner, accompanied by lots of wine, then sat around the piano with Pavarotti and his wife-to-be, Nicoletta Mantovani, and sang and laughed and drank some more. It was really a terrific evening. Pavarotti was doing what he loved doing most: singing and eating and drinking good wine.

When it was time to leave, we all shuffled into the hallway and said our good-byes. I began making my way toward the stairwell, but Pavarotti, a large man, barred my way. "No!" he bellowed. "Tonight you take the elevator!"

And I said, "You don't understand, Luciano. It's not that I don't like elevators; I just don't get in them, period."

"No! Tonight you go in elevator!"

He was a little bit drunk, and a little belligerent, and it was clear that he had no intention of letting me slip past to take the stairs. So I had a choice: I could go back into his apartment and sleep for a while, then steal away in the middle of the night like a thief. Or I could get in the elevator.

Before I could make a decision, however, Pavarotti grabbed me and dragged me into the elevator. And it wasn't a regular elevator. It was one of those tiny, old-fashioned elevators with the sliding gate and the small stool for the attendant—though of course at that time of night there was no attendant. Pavarotti then proceeded to sit on the stool, with me on his lap, and all the way to the ground floor he sang "O Sole Mio" at the top of his voice.

I have not been in an elevator since, but from that day forward, whenever I saw Pavarotti, he would always greet me in the same manner: "Hello, Elevator Man!"

Years later, I was talking about my phobia with my friend Art Janov, the *Primal Scream* guy, and he said it probably stems from having been a slightly premature baby, and from having spent the first few days of my life in an incubator. I don't know if he's right, but that's as good an explanation as any, and it beats any "previous life" theories.

The tough part is that my claustrophobia is getting worse. Lately it's gotten so bad that I can't close bathroom doors. And my greatest fear in life is that one day I'll be outside, maybe taking a hike somewhere, surrounded by mountains and babbling brooks and a crisp, cloud-dappled sky, and I'll suddenly find myself in the grip of panic. Where would I go then?

In 1999, not long after that harrowing elevator ride with Pavarotti, "The Prayer" was nominated for a Grammy. Celine and Bocelli were of course asked to perform, and Celine made it to the rehearsal, but Bocelli got stuck in Europe and I was left scrambling to find a replacement. I called my friend Seth Riggs, a wonderful voice coach, and asked him to send me a tape with a few samples. "I'm looking for people who sound like Bocelli," I said.

When the tape arrived, the first three singers were terrible. They had these big, wide, bravado voices, very Broadway, and I was looking for something palatable and silky-smooth. Then I listened to the last person on the tape and he absolutely knocked my socks off. He was singing "All I Ask from You," from *Phantom of the Opera,* and his voice was stunning. I called Seth and told him to have the kid come and see me right away.

The kid's name was Josh Groban. He was seventeen years old at the time and lived in the Hancock Park section of Los Angeles, and his parents drove him to my studio. "I want you to learn this song and I want you to come to the rehearsal at the Shrine Auditorium tomorrow," I said. "You're going to be singing with Celine Dion."

I played it through for him once, and I could see the doubt in his eyes. When it was over, he said, "I can't do it. It's too high for me." Josh is a baritone; Bocelli is a tenor.

"I know it's high for you," I replied. "But you can do it. The microphone comes past you once. You either grab hold of it or you don't. This is your moment."

I sent him on his way—the poor kid was a nervous wreck—and the next day he was back for the rehearsal. Celine was wonderful to him, immediately putting this completely unknown kid at ease. She took care of him as if she were his mother. Josh's parents were there, too, of course, and his father was filming everything with his video camera.

Then we rehearsed, and Josh was absolutely phenomenal. Everybody loved him, including Rosie O'Donnell, who would be hosting the awards that year, and who was also there to rehearse. She was really stunned by his vocal power, and the moment the song ended she called him over. "Hey, Opera Boy! Come here!" Josh walked over. "I want you on my show, kid," she said. "I need your phone number."

On the night of the Grammys, Bocelli of course showed up, and everything went flawlessly, then two months later—instant replay: The song was nominated for an Oscar, and Bocelli was again unable to make the rehearsal. Josh showed up on the morning of the Academy

Awards and again rehearsed with Celine, and he was even better than the first time. One of the producers was watching from the wings, and when it was over he came out to congratulate him. "Kid," he said, "I want you to go home and get your tux, because if Bocelli isn't here in about three hours you're going to be singing at the Academy Awards."

Bocelli showed up again, but by that point Josh was on his way. He did Rosie's show, and he was a big hit, and I later had him perform at Governor Gray Davis's inauguration, and at a fund-raiser in Los Angeles attended by Bill Clinton and a number of other political heavyweights. At that same event, I happened to run into David E. Kelley, the prolific television producer (*Picket Fences, Chicago Hope, The Practice, Ally McBeal, Boston Hope, Boston Legal*) who asked me if I would introduce him to Josh. When I brought him over, David said, "I want you to come see me. I think I have a little part for you on *Ally McBeal*."

Within a few months, we were putting the finishing touches on Josh's debut album, and Josh was also busy getting ready to make his national television debut on *Ally McBeal.* As it turned out, that was the week that Robert Downey, Jr., one of the stars of the show at the time, got busted for something or other, and suddenly Kelley and his producers were scrambling to come up with a new story line. They ended up building it around Josh. He played a geeky, goofy kid who was graduating from high school but couldn't find a date for the prom, so he asked Ally McBeal if she'd go with him. In the middle of the prom, Josh got up and sang "You're Still You" and the whole place fell completely silent. It was the television version of my real-life experience with Celine, when I first heard her sing live, in the rain, north of Montreal. The whole world just stopped.

At that point, Josh Groban had pretty much arrived. A star was born.

I finished producing Josh's album, titled, appropriately enough, *Josh Groban,* and it sold about four million units, and then I went back to work with Bocelli, who was already a global star. But Bocelli wasn't happy. He was always conflicted about pop music and decided to go back to classical. From a commercial standpoint, I didn't think that was the best move for him, but it fed his soul, and it was hard to argue with that.

Bocelli will ask for a private plane and a million bucks to show up somewhere to sing a few pop songs, but if you give him a coach-class ticket and five thousand dollars he'll fly across the world to sing opera. And he is truly amazing. He knows the repertoire, inside and out. No matter how many times I work with him, and no matter the genre, I'm always in awe of that voice. I'm a huge fan, and the fact that I'm getting paid to sit there and listen to him sing is sometimes hard to believe.

In September 2000, I was introduced to another startlingly good singer. I was invited to Montreal, to the wedding of Caroline Mulroney, the prime minister's only daughter, and Mulroney kept telling me that he had a big surprise for me. I had a big surprise for him, too. Before I flew up to Montreal, I'd had a conversation with his gorgeous wife, Mila, who told me that Mulroney was a bit of a frustrated saloon singer. (I'd seen a bit of that already, at the party at Splash.) Shortly after the guests settled in—they included the first President Bush, Queen Noor, and several other heads of state—I dragged Mulroney onto the stage and had him sing "Thank Heaven for Little Girls," accompanying him on the piano. He was a big hit.

Throughout the evening, Mulroney kept reminding me about his big surprise, and when the time came he grabbed me and said, "David, wait till you hear this guy, he's terrific!" He literally strong-armed me and dragged me to a choice spot in the front of the stage, and I remember thinking, *The prime minister has become my new talent scout.* And I said to him, "Brian, I listen to these guys all the time. That's what I *do*." And he said, "No, no, believe me. This guy you're gonna love."

Then this kid came out on stage, and he was getting ready to sing, but nobody was paying attention. It was like a scene in a movie where the wedding singer isn't getting any respect. But I stood there with Brian Mulroney, waiting, and when the kid opened his mouth—he did "Mack the Knife"—I was absolutely floored. It was like that Celine moment, that day in the rain; or the time I first heard Josh Groban at the Grammy rehearsal; or the day I listened to Andrea Bocelli's tape; or listening to the Corrs for the first time in a New York City studio: The whole world stopped, and I saw and heard nothing but that kid on stage.

His name was Michael Bublé, and he came from a family of Canadian fishermen, and he'd been doing gigs all across Canada. He had this Elvis thing going, but he was also doing lots of forties stuff, and his delivery was nothing short of phenomenal. Harry Connick, Jr. had done that kind of music, too, and he had owned the slot, just like Frank Sinatra had owned it before him, but Frank was dead and Connick was busy raising children and being a movie star. That's why I knew right away that I could make things happen for the kid.

I went up to Bublé after the show and introduced myself, and I told him we needed to be working together. Before long, he came to Malibu, where I put him up for three months and got to work. When it came time to sign him to a deal, however, I was reluctant to go to Warners with yet another new outside-the-box artist—Groban was only just starting to hit—so I went to my friend Paul Anka and asked him if he wanted to invest a half-million dollars to make the album with me. If he said yes, I told him, I would do the heavy lifting and deliver the finished album to Warners, and Paul and I would own a big piece of Mr. Bublé. Paul was interested, but he wasn't ready to commit, so I suggested it to another friend, Haim Saban, who got on board immediately.

Haim is a very close friend and an unusually gifted guy. We met more than thirty years ago, when he was a songwriter, writing music for network cartoons. At one point, early in his career, he told the networks that he would give them the music for free if he could keep the publishing rights, and that brilliant idea turned him into a millionaire many times over. He then discovered "The Mighty Morphin Power Rangers," somewhere in Asia, brought them to America, and in short order sold them for a fortune. Then he started the Fox Family Channel with Rupert Murdoch and sold that for 5.2 billion dollars. I wish I could tell you he was an asshole, but he's one of the most generous, thoughtful, and kind-hearted people I know, and I was really looking forward to being in business with him because it meant we would be spending even more time together. And who knows business better than Haim Saban?

In addition to business and entertainment, Haim and his wife, Cheryl, are very politically active. Last year, they had a big fundraiser for Hillary Clinton, when she was running for president, and Hillary told me she was a big Josh Groban fan. "It seems like people of all ages love him," she said.

"Yes," I replied with my usual tact. "Everyone from age eight to age eighty. Women don't know whether to breastfeed him or fuck him."

Hillary smiled. It was a tight smile, admittedly, but it was a smile nonetheless.

Before Haim and I even began discussing the Bublé deal, however, Josh started making waves, and I realized I could go directly to Warners without any outside investors—which is precisely what I did. And it's too bad, really. It would have been a very lucrative joint venture, and I let it slip away. It is rare for a producer to own a piece of the artist. Generally, a producer takes a cut, which works out to about fifty cents per unit. But he doesn't start seeing a penny until the label has recouped the recording costs and a portion of the marketing costs and assorted expenses, and in my experience that first fifty cents doesn't kick in until you've sold about a million units.

Even as I continued to work with Bublé, I was putting the finishing touches on Bocelli's *Cieli di Toscana,* and when we were done I was asked to appear on *Popstars,* a short-lived WB reality series about breaking in a new girl group, which I did with my sister Jaymes. The sad thing about *Popstars* is that we didn't get it quite right, because it was a good idea—*American Idol* before its time—but the one thing that came out of it is that we discovered Nicole Scherzinger, who went on to become the sizzlingly hot lead singer of the Pussycat Dolls. She was the very last of four hunderd singers we had auditioned. I liked the show so much that shortly after it got cancelled I went to HBO to pitch a *Popstars*-inspired idea about a singing competition. The show was simplicity itself, and, again, it was very *Idol*-like (but pre-*Idol,* of course): Individual singers competing for big prizes and, at the end of the season, The Crown.

When I arrived at HBO, I was told that the executive was on the fortieth floor, so I asked if she'd be kind enough to come downstairs. She wasn't exactly thrilled about this, to understate the case, but she agreed, and we had our meeting in the building's basement level, at a Subway sandwich shop. "*Popstars* was a competition between groups, but we could do it with individuals, which I think is more compelling, and it will give viewers a specific person to root for," I said. "The singers would be competing for prizes and money."

She looked at me, clearly still irritated, and said, "I don't believe competition works on television." She actually said that! I think that was the stupidest comment on the planet. Then again, I sort of understood. In Hollywood, it's really about saying *No.* The moment an executive commits to a pitch, his or her job is on the line. They have to make that idea come to life, and it's so much easier to coast along without taking any chances.

But maybe I didn't like her because she was irritated by my claustrophobia. Most people at least try to be understanding. I remember I went to Sony once to get a platinum record for one of the many albums I'd done with Celine, and everyone was supposed to meet on the thirty-fourth floor, but I just didn't have it in me to walk up thirty-four flights—so they made the presentation in the lobby. Among those in attendance was my old friend Tommy Mottola, who had become chairman of Sony Music. (I told you he was going to be running the world some day.) It was very nice of all of those busy executives to accommodate me and my phobia, though of course they couldn't complain—my work with Celine was paying most of their salaries.

Another time, when I was in New York, Howard Stern invited me to be on his show, and when I arrived at the building the guard refused to let me take the stairs. "I'm sorry, there are no stairs," he said.

"There have to be stairs," I said, and I copped some attitude—because I hear this line all the time, and it's more than a little ridiculous.

"No, sir, there are no stairs."

"There have to be stairs," I repeated more forcefully. "It's the law. You have to be able to get out of this fucking building if there's a fire."

"Yes, there are stairs, but you can't go into them because they're locked from this side."

"I understand that they're locked," I said, and then I asked him, petulantly, "Do you know *why* they're locked?"

"No, sir, I do not."

And I said, "They're locked because they don't want people going back in when there's a fire. People panic; that's why they're locked. So I need to you to get the key and let me in so that I can go upstairs and do my interview."

"I'm sorry, sir, that's against regulations," he said. Then he got a little surly: "You are not going in the stairs."

Sometimes, in these types of situations, you try to talk to someone in a position of genuine authority, and I tried, believe me, but that didn't happen either, so Howard sent a crew downstairs and they filmed my interview on the sidewalk, in front of the building. We did it live, with Howard patched in from upstairs, visible on a small monitor.

The first thing he said was, "So this elevator thing is a bunch of bullshit, right? It's just so you can get attention." (That was on a par with what my friend Paul Anka had once said: "You don't go into elevators because you're afraid to hear your own music.") Before I could even respond, however, he had moved on to the next issue: "Wow, your wife, Linda—she must be some piece of ass. Elvis! Bruce Jenner!"

And I said, "Yeah, but she's not as good a piece of ass as *your* wife, Howard."

And he loved that. Howard loves shit like that. And to answer his question, No, the "elevator thing" is not about getting attention. It's actually a huge headache. My terrific assistant, Kathy Frangetis, who has been with me for ten years, is like my own personal advance team. She always has to make sure I'm booked on a low floor, and that the hotel meeting rooms are easily accessed via the stairs. But more often than not, when I show up at a hotel, they've upgraded me to a suite on the twenty-third floor, thinking they're doing me a favor. And I always have to explain myself all over again: "No, you don't understand. I don't like elevators." And it's become such a huge problem that I've decided I'm going to see a therapist about it—a guy I met through Oprah. So who knows? I could be cured by Christmas!

When I finished my tracks for *Cieli di Toscana,* I went to work with Barbra on her 2002 *Duets* album, composing the songs she did with Josh Groban and Celine. Many years earlier, shortly after I first met

Celine, I had told her that she was such an amazing singer that she would be singing with Barbra Streisand some day, and she had laughed it off, not believing it would ever happen. And it gave me great pleasure to take Celine to Barbra's house for dinner, so they could meet for the first time and start getting better acquainted. Celine simply couldn't take her eyes off Barbra. She watched how she set the napkin on her lap; raised the fork to her mouth; watched how her hands moved. And she hung on to every word. It was wonderful. I loved the way Barbra had invited Celine into her life. She could have looked at her as direct competition, but instead she embraced her. And I felt great about it, of course, because it had always been my idea to some-day bring these two superstars together.

I've often said of Celine, *I don't know if she'll ever reach the heights that Barbra has reached, but nobody will come closer.* After all, Barbra is the whole package. She sings, she acts, she directs. But nobody on the planet will get any closer to those heights than Celine Dion. The same can be said of Bublé and Sinatra: I don't know how close Bublé will get, but no one will get closer.

A few weeks later, I ran into Kenny G, with whom I'd worked a few times, and who over the years has become a very close friend. He told me he was having a party to celebrate his tenth wedding anniversary, and said I'd be getting an official invitation in the mail, and I immediately thought of a wonderful present. "Kenny," I said, "I'm working on an album with this great new singer, Michael Bublé. I'd love for him to sing a couple songs at your party. We'll put a big band together with a bunch of horns and we'll do a medley of romantic forties stuff."

"No, thanks," Kenny said. "I don't want those guys at my party. Those are the kinds of musicians who look down on my music. It would make me too uncomfortable."

I found that really disturbing. When I sit down at the piano, what comes out is what comes out. And when Kenny lays his fingers on his sax, what comes out is what comes out. Somehow, in doing what we do, we got lucky—because it turns out that, more often than not, the masses respond enthusiastically. But every sax player on the planet seems to dislike Kenny G. They say it's because he plays "pussy" music, but the real reason is because he has sold around fifty million records, and most of those snobs are lucky to sell a thousand. It bothers me that Kenny gets criticized for the music he makes, because it is exactly the kind of music he wants to make—the music he was put on this earth to make. And it's beautiful music. He's a hell of a musician. He could bury most sax players with his speed-of-light technique. And he plays melodies, *real* melodies.

I feel the same way about my music. I haven't always been embraced by the upper echelons of the critical elite—they call it "wallpaper music" or "elevator music" or worse—but the fans love it, and, more important, *I* love it.

I also love Van Halen, Kanye West, Jay-Z, and 'N Sync. I love classical music and Pavarotti and Tim McGraw. But when I lay my hands on the piano, I play pop music, and pop stands for "popular." I'm good at it, and I don't make any excuses for it. This is the music I play and will always play, and I have no intention of stepping outside of that lane. My roots are in Rachmaninoff and jazz greats like Bill Evans, and there was a time when I didn't know any better and looked down on simple, three-chord rock, but it doesn't pay to be a snob about music. "Power ballads" and the "David Foster Sound" might not cut it for everyone, but even a guy with thirty tattoos, nose rings, earrings, and eyebrow piercings wants to make love now and then, and can he really do it to Slayer's thrash-metal "Eyes of the Insane"?

When Kenny G talked about musicians who looked down at him, I imagined a talented guy who lived in a dumpy, one-bedroom apartment in the Valley because he refused to play what people wanted to hear. I don't understand these so-called purists. There's room for all sorts of music in the world, and I've learned that even a simple C–F–G chord has plenty of dignity, especially if it's done the right way and with the right attitude.

Pop for *popular,* remember? I've somehow figured out a way to tap into what the masses respond to. And it's not as if I sit at the piano and think, *Okay, let's see what they might like . . .* I write something and, when I'm writing well, people respond. I can't be Neil Young and I can't be Coldplay, much as I might admire them, and I can't be Bruce Springsteen either, much as I might fantasize about being a rocker. I can only be who I am, and who I am is a guy who writes music that people make babies to—and I'm not going to apologize for it.

Also, if we're talking sales, I'll let you in on a little secret. When rap music first came out, it was a big deal because some of those albums were selling two million copies. To me, two million copies—back in the nineties, anyway—was a failure. Celine Dion was selling twenty-five million albums each time out, and the soundtrack to *The Bodyguard* sold more than forty million units. *Those* are numbers.

On May 11, 2002, I was invited to give the commencement address at the Berklee College of Music, in Boston. Two of my daughters, Erin and Jordan, were there, and I began on a light note: "This is my worst nightmare—two of my girls surrounded by 750 musicians." I then said a few words about myself, somehow managing to slip in the fact that I'd won fourteen Grammys, and then I spoke about the subject I've just been addressing. I said, in part: "Don't be a musical snob . . . Probably every keyboard player here today plays better than I do. And although that's impressive, it won't take you to the top. But attitude will. And if you look at every single thing that comes your way as an opportunity, that will take you to the top, too."

On the flight home I wondered if I had helped or inspired anyone. I thought it would be great if some kid would come up to me at some event some years later and say, "You know something, Mr. Foster, I was in the audience the day you spoke at Berklee, and I listened to every word you said, and it changed my life."

And you know what? Some years later a kid *did* come up to me and say almost those exact words. And then it happened again, and again, and it keeps happening.

And all I can say to that is, *Mission accomplished.*

8

Daughters and Sons

By 2002, my fraying marriage was in serious trouble, but Linda and I were in denial about the extent of our problems. We were also pretty good at faking it, so when we were out and about, doing our Hollywood power-couple thing, no one suspected that things were falling apart.

One of our biggest problems was the same problem we'd had from the very start: the challenge of blending two families.

At that point, Sara, Erin, and Jordan were all still living in Los Angeles with their mother—Sara was the oldest at twenty-one—and it seemed as if I saw less and less of them each year. They weren't happy about it, and I felt horrible about it, but I just couldn't figure out how to make things work.

I was also having trouble with Linda's boys, Brandon and Brody, who were twenty-one and nineteen at the time. I loved them both, having been part of their lives since they were four and two, but the teenage years can be tough, and I felt I had no authority in my own home. Her boys came first, her seven dogs were next on the list, and I barely managed to squeeze my way into her Top 10.

There were times when I felt like a checkbook.

Even more troubling, however, was the non-relationship between Linda and my children. For years on end I'd been hoping that all of them would make an effort, but that never happened, and these many years later I see that the fault was largely mine. It was up to me to be the glue, but I was paralyzed by guilt—and guilt is the most useless, fucked-up emotion on the planet.

Linda and I kept trying, though, and later that year we went on a terrific cruise with Haim Saban and his family, stopping in Paris on our way back. One afternoon we went to visit Nôtre Dame Cathedral, and we came across an amazing accordion player, a street musician. He was about six-four and good-looking enough to be a model, and he was playing a medley of Italian love songs that were spectacularly romantic. When he took a short break, I complimented him on his playing, and in the course of our brief conversation I learned that he was living in his car. I dropped a few francs into his open case—maybe *more* than a few, because I really felt for the guy, and because I respected his talent—and we wandered off, but a moment later I thought to myself, *That guy is really good.* The wheels were turning. I was thinking that maybe I could produce an album with him—Italian love songs on an accordion. I figured I could call the Warners office in Paris and take him into the studio and do a demo, just to get a feel for what it might sound like, and whether it would even work, and I hurried back to talk to the guy.

We started working our way back, and when we were only a few yards away we were approached by several young gypsies asking for money. So I gave them a little money, and then next thing I knew we were surrounded by maybe fifteen or twenty kids, all of them asking for money, and by the time we broke free the accordion player was gone. I ran everywhere, looking for him. I even climbed onto a double-decker bus, hoping to spot him, but he'd disappeared.

To this day I regret having lost him.

Life is full of chance and coincidence, and I still feel as if I missed out on a great opportunity for both of us. And it amazes me: Where did the guy go? How did I miss a six-foot-four guy with a big accordion case? (Then again, if you think about it, there's a six-foot-four guy running around the desert somewhere near Afghanistan, dragging a dialysis machine around, and nobody can seem to find *him*, either.)

That was actually my second visit to Paris. The first time, I was there with Paul Anka, and he took me all over the city, trying to educate me, to give me a taste for the culture. He took me to the Eiffel Tower, and to look at paintings in the Louvre, and he made me walk for hours around the Left Bank and across ancient bridges spanning the Seine. And on our final night, as a reward, he took me to a fancy restaurant, and he gave me shit because I was wearing jeans and an "ugly" shirt. I had to borrow a jacket from the maitre d' just to get fed, but it was worth it: Being with Paul is always an education.

Paul also had a favorite expression that has stayed with me to this day: "Good is the enemy of great." I firmly believe that. Anybody can be good; the challenge—in everything—is to be great.

That same year, there was more family drama, but it was the good kind. As you may recall, when I was living in Edmonton I got a girl pregnant, and she decided she couldn't keep the child. Now here I was, more than thirty years later, when I got a call from my assistant, Kathy Frangetis: She had just heard from someone in Canada who was related to a young woman who thought she was my daughter.

I don't think I was shocked, to be honest. I think I had been expecting that phone call for thirty years. Every child wants to know his or her parents, so I always suspected it would only be a matter of time.

Two days later, I was sitting on the phone at my studio in Malibu, talking with a woman who said she was that child. Her name was Allison, she told me; she was married and had two kids, and the family lived in Edmonton. We were both intensely curious about each other.

As it turned out, I had business in Edmonton not long after, with Wayne Gretzky, the hockey player, and we arranged to meet, and before we did so I subjected myself to a DNA test to make sure this was the child I'd held for a minute more than thirty years earlier. As soon as the tests confirmed our suspicions, we made arrangements to meet at the hotel where I was staying, and the moment she walked through the door any doubts I might have had were immediately dispelled: Allison looked more like me than my four other girls. Weird!

Allison had lived a full life, and she had three decades of stories to tell, and that night she began by telling me how she found me. She had heard through a cousin that her father was a famous Canadian musician, and she began to do a little research on the Internet. She came up with two possibilities, and the moment she saw the first guy's picture she knew it couldn't possibly be him. "He was about six-foot-eight and ugly," she said, laughing. Then she saw my picture and was greatly relieved. She also saw the resemblance, and after thinking about it for a few days decided to track me down through my foundation.

Minutes after we met, at that Edmonton hotel, Allison introduced me to her husband, Brent, who had been waiting in the lobby, and I found out that both he and Allison were huge—and I mean HUGE—hockey fans. I crossed the room and picked up the phone and rang Wayne, who was also staying at the hotel. "You've got to come to my room," I said. "The most extraordinary thing has just happened."

He showed up a few minutes later, and Allison's head was spinning. She was meeting her father and Wayne Gretzky on the same day, within minutes of each other. I remember the look of shock on her face. "Oh God," she was saying. "This is my dad, and this is Wayne Gretzky. I can't believe it." I think she was actually a little more excited about meeting Wayne.

Allison and her family are very much part of my life now, and it's great.

Meanwhile, I was also dealing with another Canadian, Michael Bublé, whose self-titled album we released in 2003. It was a compilation of standards from various eras, everything from "Moondance" to "For Once in My Life" to "How Can You Mend a Broken Heart." This last song was originally a big hit for Barry Gibb and the Bee Gees, and Barry actually agreed to sing backup vocals on Bublé's version. Paul Anka went out of his way to help us pick the music, despite the fact that I'd let a great investment opportunity slip through our hands.

The album first popped the charts in Canada and the United Kingdom, then hit Number One in Australia before reaching *Billboard*'s Top 50 in the United States. The following year, at the Juno Awards, Bublé won for "Best New Talent." We were also nominated for "Album of the Year."

Bublé and I have what I'll describe as a good working relationship, and we're about to do our fourth album together, but we both have moments in the studio when we get a little testy. It's only partly him, of course, and over the years I've learned that it's a good policy to acknowledge your mistakes. I remember, for example, suggesting that he consider recording a version of "Carmelita's Eyes," the Neil Diamond song that had always been a big favorite of mine. When I played it for him in the studio, however, I realized it wasn't very good at all, and I thought back to that period in my life—I had just left Rebecca for

Linda—and to how badly my judgment had been impaired by my personal drama. Live and learn, I guess.

Then I got a call from a friend in Canada who told me that my old employer, Ronnie Hawkins, was apparently dying of pancreatic cancer. I felt awful and decided to fly to Toronto and rent a room in a hotel and throw a big party for him, and the first guy I called was Bill Clinton. I'd met Clinton on the fundraising circuit, as well as at a number of Hollywood parties, and I knew he was a fan of Ronnie's. Ronnie had started out in Arkansas, Clinton's home state, and Clinton had often watched him perform.

Now that I think of it, I actually jammed once with Clinton at one of those Hollywood parties. He loves music, but he isn't much of a musician. On the other hand, from the few conversations I've had with him over the years, I can tell you unequivocally that he is one of the smartest people I've ever met. He knows almost everything about everything, or seems to, anyway, and that's pretty seductive. Also, when he's talking to you, he breaks the eighteen-inch rule and tends to get in your face, but he seems so genuinely interested that you feel like the only person in the room, and when the conversation ends you float away, charmed and smitten.

I wish I had a bit of more of that. I could use that in the studio with some of my artists.

Ronnie's party was basically my way of giving my old friend a chance to talk about his life, and to regale us with stories, and his stories were nothing short of mesmerizing. It was the only time in my life that I saw Bill Clinton say absolutely nothing for four hours straight. He just sat there quietly taking notes, hanging onto every gem that came out of Ronnie's mouth, and I learned later that a friend of his was dying of pancreatic cancer, and that he hoped to cheer him up with some of Ronnie's saltier stories.

The party turned out to be a huge success, and my one regret is that I had invited my mother along, but only because Ronnie got a little wild. At one point he turned to my mother and said, "Ma'am, I'm getting ready to tell a bunch of X-rated stories for these heathens. Maybe you better leave." And she said, "I wouldn't leave for a thousand dollars!" So Ronnie plunged right in: "Then I got this bitch up on her knees and took her from behind!" "I had these two hookers going down on each other on top of the dinner table!" "She was screaming for more, and I kept saying, 'Girl, that's all I got'!"

I had about fifty people there, including Paul Anka, and it was beautifully catered, but Ronnie might have been a tad disappointed—nobody went down on anyone or took anyone from behind or screamed for more (not while I was there with my mother, anyway).

Months later, Ronnie was still alive. He claimed that he had been to see a healer in Vancouver, and that the cancer had gone into remission, and maybe it's true. But maybe he never had cancer at all. You never know with Ronnie. Still, he's a great guy, so he can get away with all sorts of shit. If it was a publicity stunt, it was a good one, and—whatever it was—I'm glad he's still alive.

That Christmas, my old friend Barry DeVorzon invited Linda and me to a small party at his house in Santa Barbara. (Barry is the guy who fell in love with "Wildflower" back in the early seventies, and brought Skylark to Los Angeles.) I asked him if I could bring Renee Olstead, a young singer I'd just signed—I always do everything I can to put my artists in the limelight—and Barry was a little hesitant. Oprah was going to be one of the guests, and he didn't want to mix business with pleasure. Still, after giving it some thought, he told me I should go ahead and bring Renee, and that we'd ask her to sing if the circumstances were right.

I wanted very much to do this for Renee. I'd been introduced to her by a friend who had initially approached me to try to sell me a song for Josh Groban, but I didn't respond to it and she took it very well. "Okay, fine," she said. "You don't like my song, that's cool. But I'm going to introduce you to a singer that is so incredibly talented you are not going to believe your ears." She left me a CD, and I was blown away. The girl was thirteen years old and was singing standards with incredible force and feeling. I invited her to the studio, just to make sure she was real, and before long Humberto and I produced her first album. It did not do well—by my standards, anyway—and this was for two simple reasons: One, she was working on a network show called *Still Standing* and was contractually barred from doing any publicity. And two, it was a little disconcerting to listen to a young teenager sing racy songs about wanting to kiss and love her man, etc.

When we got to Barry's place, for the little party, Renee hung out in the kitchen—I wanted this to be a surprise—and I went off to be introduced to Oprah. I'm sure she knew absolutely nothing about me, but within seconds she made me feel as if I were the most fascinating man on the planet. (She and Bill Clinton have that gift in common. Most people are lost in a bottomless black hole of self-absorption, but people like Oprah and Bill make you feel as if you are the most important and fascinating person they've ever had the pleasure of meeting.) When I told Oprah that the Beatles had been one of my early influences, she wanted to know why, and she was dead serious about it. She wasn't just going through the motions. And it reminded me of an old saying: "If you find yourself interesting, you're a bore. But if you find *me* interesting, you're a genius."

By the time we sat down to dinner, I knew Oprah was a genius, and I was absolutely crazy about her. And after dinner, with Barry's blessing, I went off to get Renee. "I don't know if I can do this!" she said. "It's like meeting God." But she went out and she did it, and Oprah loved her—and two weeks later she had her on the show. The girl was an instant hit.

· · ·

As the New Year got underway, I had still more success with Josh Groban's second album, *Closer,* but our relationship was becoming increasingly complicated. I was under the impression that Josh was just a beautiful voice, and that I could push him around a bit and tell him what to do, but he was a lot deeper, musically, than I'd given him credit for. On his first album, he listened to me and trusted my choices. On *Closer,* however, he was coming up with ideas of his own. In due course, I discovered that he played piano, was good on drums, liked writing songs, and was into Radiohead, Dave Matthews, and Imogen Heap—all of this quirky stuff that wasn't on my radar. One day in the studio he did a perfect impression of Eddie Vedder, from Pearl Jam, which was really quite brilliant, and followed that up by doing *all* the voices from *South Park,* but despite my admiration for Josh's many talents, I was worried that we might be moving in different directions.

I also worked with Celine that year, on *Miracle,* but I wasn't as focused as I would have liked to be. Linda and I were continuing to have problems, and at one point I had an affair and left home for three months. We should have separated, but instead we got back together and I agreed to go into couples therapy.

Therapy turned into one of the most unpleasant experiences of my life. It boiled down to several months of David-bashing: All we talked about was my affair, and what a horrible husband I'd been, but at least I learned two things during those sessions. The first was that I might *seem* like a romantic guy, but that I have a tendency to put all of that romance into my music. (Perhaps that's why I was on my third marriage.)

The second was even more revealing: In one of the sessions, it suddenly occurred to me that my father had never told me that he loved me, and for some reason I found this devastating. Neither of my parents were particularly emotive people, as I've said, and I know they loved me by the way they treated me, but it would have been nice to hear them say it. My father was long gone, and for a time I wondered whether I should broach this whole touchy-feely subject with my aging mother, but she passed away in January 2006, so we never discussed it.

That summer, Brody and Brandon and their friend Spencer Pratt began running around the Malibu compound with video cameras, documenting their shenanigans, and every time they pointed the cameras at me I'd give them the finger and tell them to get out of my face. It was a joke—I was just messing around, screaming like a crazy person—but it soon got tiresome, and before long I was screaming at them in earnest. They then told me that they were going to try to sell a reality show about a pair of cool, privileged pranksters and their hapless, ever-exploited stepdad, and that they were going to use the videos to do so.

Several weeks later, the boys sat me down and showed me some of the rough footage. They had a segment where I was yelling at Brody for always parking his car in my spot—a minor issue, yes, but not if it happens every day. They also had footage of Michael Bublé and Brandon golfing on the lawn and bouncing balls against my studio, and of me coming out and yelling at them. (I seemed to be doing a lot of yelling.) And they had crazy shots of themselves at the beach, surfing and flirting with girls.

After we looked at the videos, the boys told me they were going to show the footage to their friend David Chernin, son of Peter Chernin, the president and chief operating officer of News Corporation, which owns the Fox studio.

"If we sell the show, will you be in it?" Brody asked me.

And Spencer got right into it, really pushing me to do it. "Come on, David. This is going to be a huge hit. Please say yes."

I thought this was laughable—I didn't think anything could possibly come of it—but I said I was game. "If it actually happens, and you get a job out of it, and you make your own money finally, yes—I'll be in it," I said.

Then I started getting into it. I suggested that they edit the rough footage into a few usable minutes—a sort of highlight/sizzle reel—and I made a call to Brant Pinvidic, the only guy I knew in the reality television business. They ended up with a great three-minute clip, which they took to David Chernin, who showed it to his dad. The next thing I knew I had signed on to a reality show called *The Princes of Malibu.*

I had seriously mixed feelings about the show from the start, but the idea was so crazy that I found it strangely appealing. More important, I had given the boys my word, and my word is everything. If I balked, there would have been no show, and this obviously meant a lot to them.

So I decided to let the cameras into our home, and on the first day it occurred to me that all of the stuff I'd been struggling with in my personal life was soon going to be on public display. And in a strange way, I actually *welcomed* the idea: The show was going to give me an opportunity to vent about all the things at home that were making me crazy.

When the crews arrived and started filming, it took a bit of getting used to, and in the beginning we were all playing to the cameras. But after they'd been around for a couple of days, we began to forget that they were there, and our truer selves emerged, and at that point I was getting genuinely angry about everything—from always finding one of the boys in my parking spot, to the family's disregard for my hard-earned money, to the blatant disrespect I got in what was supposed to be my castle. Linda was trying hard to look good for the cameras, and she continued to play to them, but the one thing she couldn't hide was the way she enabled her two boys. *They've got to eat somewhere, why not Nobu at $700 a night—sushi is healthy. They need new surfboards/new* *cars/more money/the best scuba gear (and a private instructor to go with it)/etc.* In that sense, the television wasn't lying. In fact, it was documenting critical elements of our real lives.

By the end of the first week, I discovered that the whole reality-show experience was actually having a beneficial effect—it was beginning to wake me up. I loved my wife and I loved her boys, but none of it was working. I thought about this for weeks on end, long after the film crews had gone home, and realized I wanted out, but I didn't know how—or didn't have the courage—to make my move.

Then June 22 rolled around, our anniversary, and I took Linda to dinner at Koi, a Japanese restaurant on La Cienega Boulevard, in Los Angeles. In the middle of dinner we got into a silly argument. A close friend of mine had been having an affair, and I'd known about it for many months, but I hadn't shared that knowledge with Linda, and this upset her to no end. The affair had just come to light, and Linda couldn't come to terms with the fact that I'd known about it from the start. The argument escalated until I'd had enough, and in the middle of dinner I got up, went outside, and hailed a cab, and when I got back to Malibu I slept in the guesthouse.

I didn't talk to Linda for the next three weeks, until July 10, the night the show aired, and even then we didn't talk. She and the boys had arranged a little party, and a bunch of friends had come over to watch the premiere episode, and I felt obliged to make an appearance. I had already seen the show—the producers had sent us an early version on DVD—so I didn't pay much attention, but being around the family again weakened my resolve. I didn't understand why I was living in my own guesthouse. If I was still there, maybe there was a reason for it, and maybe I needed to try to make the marriage work. I was incredibly conflicted, so I left the party early and went back to the guesthouse.

A couple of hours later, a friend called. "You need to go online, to the Fox Web site," he said. "You're not going to believe what they're saying about the show."

I booted up my computer and logged onto the site, and there must have been 400 comments from viewers. A few of them said things like, "God, David Foster is an idiot. How could he stoop to do such a moronic show?" A few more said, "This is the dumbest show in the world, and I'm not watching it again." But 390 of the 400 responses were actually sympathetic. "That poor man," people wrote. "He needs to get out of that house right now." That was the biggest epiphany of my life. I don't know how to describe it exactly, except to say that it felt as if God was speaking to me. I imagine that most of us reach a point in our lives where we wish our father or our grandfather or someone who has passed on, or God even—anyone with answers, basically—would appear at the foot of our bed and tell us, in no un-certain terms, what we were doing right and what we were doing wrong. "That thing you did last Tuesday, uh-uh—that was bad. But that thing you did Thursday, that was good." Not just a little guid-ance, but some definitive answers. And that's what I felt that night; I felt as if God was actually talking to me, lighting the way. He was standing at the foot of my bed, saying, "You're right, buddy. You don't belong here. It's a bad deal. Get out."

I never went back to Linda. The next day I phoned her from the guesthouse and told her I was going to file for divorce, and on Mon-day she beat me to it and filed first.

The same day—not that we had anything else on our minds—we heard from Fox. The show was getting great ratings, they said.

The second and third week, as I slowly adjusted to the not alto-gether unpleasant idea of my third divorce, the numbers started to drop, and the show got pulled. But at the end of the day, what did it matter? The show was over, and it had done wonders for me: It had given me the courage to end my marriage.

Oddly enough, *The Princes of Malibu* ended up being quite a big hit in Canada. When I go to Canada now, young people come up to me and say, "Dude, I want to be your kid!" I thought that was pretty funny.

It was during this period that I began to reconnect with my daughters. I was on my own, and I finally had time for them, and I was eager to get to know them better and to try to repair some of the damage I'd done through my periods of self-absorption. It's not as if I hadn't seen them, or as if I'd neglected them, but I didn't see enough of them, and I wanted to make up for lost time. I remember that I used to love to take them skiing, because I would take turns with each of them on the lift, and I could really communicate with them during those ten or fifteen or twenty minutes on our way back to the top of the mountain. Now I didn't have to wait for ski vacations. The three girls I'd had with Rebecca were right there, in Los Angeles, where they'd been all along.

Sara was twenty-four at the time—this was in 2005—and out of all my daughters she's the one who avoided the drama in my life by distancing herself, and by turning her friends into her family. At the time, I found it troubling, but I eventually realized that she was doing it to avoid getting hurt. She was always the strong one, Sara. When she was twelve, I remember telling her that she was the daughter I could have dropped in Manhattan with ten dollars, knowing she would survive and thrive. In later years, she always insisted on doing everything for herself. When she decided to try her hand at modeling, she never asked me to call an agent or a manager—she did it all on her own. She flew off to Europe at sixteen and six months later she had a ten-page photo spread in *Vanity Fair*, and after that she was booking stuff left and right. One day I asked her if I could meet her agent, and the three of us went for coffee, and all I said was, "Please take care of my daughter." I don't even know why I did that—I'm a parent, and I worry—since she was clearly very good at taking care of herself.

A couple of years later, she was acting, making her big-screen debut in *The Big Bounce,* with Owen Wilson and Morgan Freeman. She followed that up with a role in *D.E.B.S.,* a film about crime-fighting schoolgirls, and has two more features in the can. And she did it all on her own, without any help from me.

My next daughter, Erin, is the writer in the family. She's twenty-five now, and has been writing restaurant reviews and short pieces about hot new clubs for trendy magazines. She is also an actress. She's been on *Gilmore Girls, House, American Dreams, The O.C.,* and *CSI: Crime Scene Investigation.* (She always seems to get booked on shows I love.) More recently, her agent began sending her out on commercials, and she told him, "Look, I'm five-seven. I'm never going to be five-eleven. Don't send me to auditions with all those glamazons." But she goes, happily, and always enjoys the process. She is also about to launch a very cool Web site about the acting profession. Stay tuned. It's going to be big. I know my daughter.

Erin is the old soul in the family, and I often go to her for advice. I don't always take it, but I always listen. She should be writing an Ann Landers-style column geared toward kids of her generation—she's that smart. In the early years, she was the edgy one in the family, but it always worked for her—and it still does.

Jordan, next in line, is the adventurer in the family. She went off to boarding school in the tenth grade and has never stopped traveling. She lived in Colorado and New York and spent time in Africa and Alaska and Fiji. She's curious about everything. She has a real hunger for knowledge. And she is absolutely fearless. She's the most independent one in the family, and she currently lives with her boyfriend, in Zurich—she happens to have a gift for languages (first Spanish, now

German)—so she's the one I see the least. But she's happy there. She's working for a marketing company and has a great head for business. I know she's going to do great things in the corporate world.

(I remember inviting all three of them to the house one night, not long after I left the Malibu compound, to show them two boxes filled with videotapes. Like my father before me, I had made hours and hours of film of my children, and watching those tapes with my three girls at my side made me think that I wasn't such a terrible father after all.)

My other daughter, Amy, my eldest—the one I had with B.J. in 1973—lives in Nashville with her two children. Unfortunately she got a little shortchanged in the parenting department. As you may recall, B.J. took her with her to Toronto when she was only five, and back then I thought parenting boiled down to a weekly phone call and a monthly check. And of course in retrospect I see how hard it must have been for her: I was living in Los Angeles with Rebecca and three girls, and she was an only child, in far-off Toronto, missing her father. But she has thrived. She's a successful lyricist—a gift she inherited from her mother. She wrote "Because We Believe," a song I did with Bocelli, and she wrote "Home," which was a huge hit for Michael Bublé—and which I had nothing to do with. She's also writing an intricate, deeply layered novel about female friendships, and the few parts she's let me read are absolutely amazing. And she's already found a publisher, so clearly I'm not the only one who thinks so.

Allison, my surprise daughter, the one I gave up for adoption, remains in Edmonton, with her husband Brent and their two sons. She works as an executive for a computer company and is actually taking time from her busy schedule to help me with my next fundraiser, which will be in Edmonton. It's a rewarding relationship and it gets better everyday.

I look at these girls, and all I want is for them to do well. At the end of the day it's the only thing you really give a shit about. And I've helped them, but I've been careful about helping them—I don't believe in this trust-fund crap. I helped each of them with the down payment on modest apartments, and I helped each of them with their first cars (Volvos as opposed to flashy BMWs). And it has really worked. All of them know and understand the value of money. So, yes, they definitely grew up in a fairly privileged environment, but they were never spoiled.

At the end of the day, the weeks and months following the disintegration of my third marriage were a very interesting time in my life. My life with Linda was over, but I was reconnecting with my family. And before long I realized that the damage was not irreparable.

Meanwhile, I kept working. Or trying to, anyway. Before *The Princes of Malibu* aired, I'd started working with Josh Groban on his third album, *Awake,* but I ended up not producing the whole thing. I was dealing with my crumbling marriage, and before long I was conferring with divorce attorneys, and the stress made it very hard to focus. Josh had to find other producers, and his manager, my friend Brian Avnet, was completely understanding.

I think at some point all artists with genuine talent need to do music that comes from them, not simply the music that the producer asks them to consider. They need to feed their souls, too.

And I have such faith in Josh's talent that I know he'll make the right choices in the years ahead. In fact, not long after I met him, I remember telling him, "One day there won't be room for me in your life. You'll be producing yourself."

That's always the balancing act in this business: Art and commerce tend to be natural enemies, but you can't push commerce at the expense of art. Think about it: If I had discovered Madonna, and I was her producer, would I still be making her do disco?

I got busy with other projects. I appeared as a mentor on *Ameri-*

can Idol, which is of course where I met Katherine McPhee, and I brought Andrea Bocelli with me. Bocelli was quite impressed with Katherine. "She has a wonderful voice," he said. "And she's also very beautiful."

"Beautiful?" I said. "How would you know?"

"Don't worry," Bocelli said. "I just know."

I also remember being very unhappy with Simon Cowell's assessment of one of Katherine's performances—it was actually one of my Whitney songs, "I Have Nothing"—and I caught up with him afterward, backstage. "Simon," I said, "I usually agree with you, but I think you were wrong about that performance. It was flawless."

"Really?" he said. "I disagree."

The next day he apologized to Katherine. Maybe he thought about what I'd said and had a change of heart.

I also remember the first time Katherine came out to my studio, in Malibu. She was doing "Over the Rainbow" and hit a bum note, and I said, "You call that singing?" Another artist might have been offended, but Katherine took a beat and smiled, and that's just one of the many things I love about her: She can take a little friendly abuse, and she'll keep working on the song until it's perfect.

Some weeks later I did a stint on *The View* as Star Jones's vocal coach. This last gig was really to let the audience in on some tricks of the trade. We wanted to see if I could use my skills, along with a lot of technology, to take a moderately talented singer, like Star Jones, and make her sound like the real thing. It took a few passes, but this is the digital era, and it allows for a lot of manipulation, and by the time we were done Star was belting out a pretty good version of "I Will Always Love You."

I kept working. In work, there was escape.

Then Bocelli called. He wanted to do another album with me, and I think I know why: Bocelli had distanced himself from pop music and had inadvertently made room for Josh Groban. I believe Josh's phenomenal success made him reconsider, and it was a good thing, too . . .

Bocelli and I subsequently locked ourselves in the studio, and—with the help of Humberto and Tony Renis—produced his next album, *Amore*. It went on to sell four million copies, putting him back at the top of the pop world. Then we went to Lake Las Vegas and put on an extravaganza called "Under the Desert Sky," which was in effect the visual version of that album. It was subsequently turned into a PBS television special, and made for an unusual show: Bocelli performed on a 4,000-square-foot floating stage. The stage—the entire community, in fact—had been the brainchild of Ron Boeddeker, who two decades earlier had arrived in this desert community, some seventeen miles from the Las Vegas Strip, and built the place from scratch.

That leaves the Big Question unanswered: At what point should a star change lanes? Early, like Joss Stone? Late, like Bocelli? Annually, like Madonna and Elton John? Or never, like Celine?

Sometimes it's hard for an artist to listen, especially if he or she is successful. Many of them are surrounded by people who spend the better part of the day telling them how wonderful they are, and they begin to believe it, and before long they're convinced they can do no wrong. It happens to everyone. Musicians. Movie stars. *Record producers!* The more successful we become, the less input we think we need from others. Artists stop listening because they think they know better, and as they begin to make their own choices their careers generally begin to suffer. There are exceptions, of course—Celine, for example, whose faith in her team has never wavered, and who never wanders far from what she does best; and Michael Bublé, who has stayed in his lane and *owns* it—but some of them will fight you tooth and nail for every square inch of real estate, and you do battle the best way you know how.

And you pick your battles. I'm drawn to artists when I believe I can help them in a significant way; I want my contribution to really count for something. I remember running into Stevie Wonder not long after he released *Natural Wonder,* and we discussed the possibility of working together—something we'd done three or four times already. "If you really want to make this happen," I said, "you can sing the songs any way you like, two times, but then you have to sing it my way *six* times." I thought he was surrounded by yes men; he didn't have anyone around to remind him of his greatness.

"What about my last album?" he asked. "Didn't you love it?"

"Stevie," I said, "your last album sucked! We can do a great album together. I have a clear vision of where you can be musically."

He never called.

Then I did *Celebrity Duets* for Fox, which was produced by the *American Idol* team, but it didn't fly. Little Richard, Marie Osmond, and I were the judges. We watched real singers team up with celebrity singers, and it was fun, but it didn't get good ratings. We had a lot of great people on the show—Al Jarreau, James Ingram, Peter Frampton, Jeffrey Osborne, etc.—and we put them on stage with every celebrity who thought he or she could sing. I'm sorry, Cheech Marin, singing isn't your strong suit. Keep your day job. It was tough to say this on a couple of counts: Cheech is a friend of mine, and—his limited range notwithstanding—he loves to sing.

Meanwhile, I was struggling through other, more personal battles, and there were times when they really wore me down. Once the divorce lawyers got seriously involved, the madness started. Linda's team was arguing that I had been a producer of middling talent when she met me, and that in the course of our long marriage she had been instrumental in propelling my career to new heights. She was asking for a huge percentage of my future earnings. My own lawyers responded:

Mr. Foster was already a successful music producer when he met Linda, and perhaps he has become better known in the past decade, but whatever fame he has never generated a penny for him. He earns his money with his brain and with his hands, as he has done since he was a teenager.

I have to tell you, I hate divorce lawyers. Criminal lawyers see the worst people on their best behavior; divorce lawyers see the best people on their worst behavior (and take advantage of them every step of the way). And then of course there are *entertainment* lawyers, like my very own Alan Grubman, who has seen me at my best *and* at my worst, and who continues to take care of me with great care and great style. I love him for a lot of reasons, but mostly because he's got brass balls.

During this period, not wanting to think about my divorce, or about the life I'd left behind, I began dating casually—*very* casually. I may be a hopeless romantic, but at this stage, with three failed marriages behind me, I figured I was done.

That summer, I was at a party at Quincy Jones's house and ran into Mohammed Hadid, a very talented architect and builder. I'd met him a few weeks earlier, at a small dinner party hosted by my good friends Ray and Ghada Irani, and that night at Quincy's he told me he was having a party of his own the following week, and he gave me directions to his house in Bel Air. It was a spectacular house—Hadid had designed and built it himself—and everywhere I looked there were photographs of a beautiful woman.

"Who is that?" I asked him.

"That's Yolanda," he said. "My ex-wife."

I thought that was very unusual. If I have any pictures of any of my ex-wives, I'm sure they're in boxes, not on display, but Mohammed and Yolanda were that rare couple who somehow remained friendly— *close*, even—after the divorce.

God, I wish I was that evolved.

Two weeks later, Mohammed invited me back to his house for another party, with the intention of introducing me to his ex-wife, but she didn't show up, and he subsequently called to tell her that she had really blown it. "There was a guy here I wanted to introduce you to," he said.

I thought that was unusual, too. This man wanted to introduce me to his ex-wife?

Yolanda also found this unusual. She lived in Santa Barbara, with their three children, and it wasn't always convenient to make the hour-and-a-half drive to Los Angeles, which is why she hadn't shown up—she was busy being a mother—but suddenly she was curious, and she made an effort and came to Mohammed's next party. I was there with a date, and when Yolanda walked over to introduce herself I was immediately smitten (much to my date's chagrin).

The next day I phoned Yolanda and reached her on her cell. She was horseback riding with the kids, who are serious equestrians, as is she, and she kept interrupting the conversation to shout commands: "Watch the jump!" "Keep your toes up!" etc.

In the middle of this conversation, having found out she was from Holland, I told her I spoke fluent Dutch—which isn't true—and I passed the phone to my genius programmer, co-musician, and right-hand man, Jochem vanderSaag, who really is from Holland, and he immediately started speaking to her in flawless Dutch. They went on at length, and he was pretending to be me and saying all sorts of crazy things: "Yes, my accent is flawless—I lived in a Dutch monastery for two years." Just having a little fun with her. And then he passed the phone back to me and Yolanda was practically swooning. "Oh my God," she was saying. "I had no idea you spoke Dutch! Why did you keep this from me at the party? This is unbelievable! You speak my language and you understand my culture!" And I said, "No, Yolanda, it was a joke. That wasn't me, it was a friend of mine." But she didn't hear me because she was distracted with the kids. "Looser! Watch your lead!"

I didn't talk to her until the next day, many hours after she'd reached her mother in Holland. "Mom," she had told her. "I have met the man of my dreams! I love the way he looks, I love his eyes, and—best of all—he's Dutch! He speaks Dutch fluently and he knows and understands our culture." And her mother said, "You've finally come to your senses, Yolanda! You're going to be with a nice Dutch boy!"

A few days later I went to Santa Barbara to take her out to dinner—she was well worth the long drive—and of course I had to admit I wasn't Dutch. I also admitted that I'd been dating indiscriminately since my divorce, which I don't think impressed her too much, but we got beyond that, and the next thing I knew we had become a bona fide couple in love.

She may be the most spectacular woman I have ever met.

And one of the most amazing things about Yolanda is the way she went out and immediately began helping me mend fences with my daughters. She changed all of our lives in ways I can't even begin to describe. Everyone in the family is madly in love with her, and we decided, unanimously, to make her president of the Foster Family.

After three failed marriages, I'm beginning to think that the idea of spending your entire life with one person only works if you know that you're going to get crushed to death by a herd of stampeding dinosaurs by the age of twenty. Still, at age fifty-eight, I'd like to think I'll be spending the rest of my life with Yolanda, and I can only hope the feeling is mutual. I know my daughters are crazy about her, because I've already been warned: *If the relationship doesn't work out, we're going with her, not you.*

Even Yolanda jokes about it. "If your father and I ever break up," she says to my daughters, "take me with you."

Meanwhile, with my divorce from Linda grinding slowly forward, and with the divorce lawyers happily lining their pockets, I sold the Malibu compound—my *Bodyguard* house—with the stipulation that I could continue to work at my studio on the property for the next two years. That didn't happen, however, because the Malibu fires came along. The main house was spared, but the studio was all but destroyed.

That same year, we released Michael Bublé's *Call Me Irresponsible*. Michael and I had occasionally battled over his choices. I love him, but his earlier successes were making him a little too overconfident and he pushed me to include a number of tracks that I felt were wrong for him. But Michael was not unhappy. He chose tracks that reflected what he wanted to do, not what his producer thought he should do, and he was more than pleased with the result.

Still, every producer I talk to always whines about the "corrupting" influence of success. With the first couple of albums, we get a lot of "Yes, sir—whatever you want, sir." By the third or fourth, it's more like "No, no—that's not for me. Let's do it this way."

And it cuts both ways: I've heard plenty of artists whine about successful producers. Maybe familiarity does breed contempt; maybe producers should never do more than two or three albums with any given artist.

Still, as I've learned, that's the process, and the important thing is not to take it personally. But I honestly believe that the more control the artist has, the poorer the album tends to perform. As an artist, I try to respect his or her choices, but as a producer—and, hence, a businessman—I have to think about commerce. You win some, you lose some. And sometimes you win but you still lose.

A case in point: The year 2007 saw the release of *The Best of Chicago–40th Anniversary Edition.* In the album's liner notes, I, David Foster, was described by members of the band as "an egomaniac who wants to do everything himself . . . and wants his name on everything." I guess I could have let them put thirteen crappy songs on a crappy album, but I was producing it and I wasn't going to let that happen. As I've said, compromise breeds mediocrity.

And really, the numbers speak for themselves. When we started working together, Chicago had just come off an album that sold 100,000 copies, a crushing disappointment by any stretch of the imagination. *Chicago 16,* my first album with them, sold two and a half million copies; and *Chicago 17,* our next effort, sold seven million copies. The band is currently living off my contribution, so I don't know what they're whining about. Then again, Lee Loughnane, the band's trumpet player, subsequently changed his tune (sort of). "[A]s it turns out, the producers that we had the most trouble with, we had the best success with," he said.

From 100,000 to two and a half million to seven million. Hmm.

Even though the criticism stung, there are ten good reviews for every bad one. And as I've said, I try not to pay attention to reviews, good or bad. Who needs 'em? I've had four pretty good decades.

In November 2007, Josh Groban and I appeared on Oprah's annual "Favorite Things" episode, and a month later his holiday CD, *Noël*— which I arranged and produced—was on its way to becoming one of the top-selling Christmas albums of all time, eventually selling close to four million copies in just three months. Those numbers mean something, by the way, especially in today's dwindling marketplace.

I remember getting an e-mail from Oprah that Christmas, she'd received a rough cut of the album from me when it was still a work in progress. She was in South Africa and wrote to tell me that she had forgotten her copy of *Noël.* "I was going to ask you to send me a copy, but I found a store here that had it—my favorite Christmas album! Now I can listen to my Josh every day!" Oprah had been introduced to Josh by her friend Gayle King, who may well be Josh's Number One Fan.

Then I got more good news: *Call Me Irresponsible* won the Grammy for Best Traditional Pop Album, which I shared with my partner on the project, Humberto Gatica.

As I said, sometimes you win, and sometimes you lose—and sometimes everybody wins.

It was an especially sweet victory, since I hadn't won a Grammy since 1996—and ten years between Grammys is a very long time indeed. I'm sure very few people were aware of this, but I sure as hell was.

9
Decade No. 5

In 2000, during the AOL merger with Time-Warner, I was talking to Steve Case, then chairman of AOL, and he predicted the future: "This record business is a very strange business," he said. "You guys invest tens of millions of dollars to turn people into stars, and all you have to show for it is a shiny, round plastic disc that will soon be completely worthless."

He was absolutely right. The record industry today is like the *Titanic* after the collision with the iceberg. The band is still playing, and people are sitting in their deck chairs, but no amount of misguided optimism is going to keep the ship from going down. Record companies are going to have to start partnering with their artists, and sharing in *all* the revenue. It makes no sense, for example, for the record company to spend anywhere from three to five million dollars to create a superstar, then get nothing in return beyond dwindling CD sales. The manager gets a piece, the agent gets a piece, and the lawyer gets a piece, and certainly the record company is entitled to a piece.

If Justin Timberlake goes off and makes a ten-million-dollar Pepsi commercial, for example, the record company—the company that helped make him a star—should be entitled to a piece of the action. (Of course, I'm speaking as a record executive here, not as a musician. If I were speaking as an artist, I would probably tell the record companies to take a hike.)

But it's a little sad, really. One of the telling problems with the music business these days is that when you walk through the halls of the record companies *you don't hear any music being played.* Back in the old days, music would be pounding from every room. You'd go into Clive Davis's office, or Tommy Mottola's office, or Doug Morris's office, or Edgar Bronfman's office, and you'd hear music blasting day and night. People would be saying, "Turn that shit down!" But I loved it—we all did: We were *listening* to music, which is what it's all about. Nowadays, though, you don't hear a sound. Now it's just numbers. It's just guys looking at computer screens to see how the album is doing, or *not* doing—which is usually the case.

Strangely enough, while the record business is in the toilet, the *music* business itself is thriving. It is bursting with cool, creative energy, and as I move into the next phase of my career I'm going to be "drilling down" for the next breakout artist. People everywhere will always hunger for great songs, songs that move them, and the challenge for me, as I begin my fifth decade in the music business, is to keep looking for new talent.

Katherine McPhee is a case in point. She was only a runner-up on the fifth season of *American Idol,* but she has the voice of an angel, and I'm confident I can help her carve out the career she deserves. We are currently working on her next album.

I'm happy to keep working with superstars, certainly, but few things bring me as much pleasure as developing a new artist, or help-ing an artist rediscover him- or herself, and then sharing the results with the world. Still, if I have one small regret about my career, it's that I didn't pour more of my energy into discovering new talent. I found it more appealing and more seductive to work with established artists—*easier,* too—and I sometimes wonder what would have hap-pened if I'd done the hard work it takes to create stars.

Maybe I would have brought *ten* Celines into the world . . .

But I'm working on it. William Joseph, a piano player with the fastest hands on the planet, is a good example. I like to describe him as a younger, more handsome version of me—and a better piano player, too. Sometimes I wonder whether I'm attracted to him because he's going to have the kind of career I wanted but never got. Back in the day, I fancied myself as the next Henry Mancini or Burt Bacharach or John Williams, but I never went down that road, so now I do it vicari-ously through my various artists. It's like being the parent of a talented child: "That's my kid! Isn't he great?"

I met William some years ago, in Phoenix, while I was working on a fundraiser for Muhammad Ali. Somebody came up to me during a break in the rehearsals and said they wanted to introduce me to a local pianist, a kid who got his start through a local chapter of the Boys and Girls Club. When they brought William over, I asked him to play a little something, and he said, "Can I play a song I wrote?" And I said, "Sure." He sat down and pounded out an incredible tune, and because the musicians were still on stage, listening, I waved an imaginary baton and had them join in. It was incredible. I was shocked at how good he was.

When he finished, everyone applauded, and I marched over to his side and said, "You know what? Normally I open the show, on piano, but tonight you're going to open the show." It was another one of those great moments in my life, like the time I went up to Josh Groban and told him, "You're going to be singing with Celine Dion."

He opened the show and got a standing ovation, and I knew there was definitely a slot for him in the music business. He would be to piano what Kenny G was to sax. I figured people were ready for instrumentals again, and I thought—and still think—that William was the guy to reintroduce them. If he had played classical music, I couldn't have done anything for him, despite his enormous talent. But he's a pop crossover—a Groban or a Bocelli (without the vocals)—and we're going to crack the code.

I'm also working with Peter Cincotti, a phenomenal jazz pianist. His debut album came out right about the time we released Bublé's first album, and I've been watching him ever since. You know the old phrase: "Keep your friends close and your enemies closer"?

This was back in 2001. Peter was just shy of twenty at the time, and he was on my radar from the very start. Then I went off to do Renee Olstead's album and asked him if he would sing a duet with her. He did, and he was terrific. He played piano the way I always wanted to play piano but never could.

Not long after I got a call from Tom Whalley—the chairman of Warner Bros. Records, my boss, effectively—and he said, "I know you love this guy Peter Cincotti. He's leaving his label, Concord, and there's a chance we could sign him. Would you be interested?"

"Yes," I said. "I would be very interested."

"Good," Whalley said. "But there's something you should know. Peter has changed directions."

I thought, *Okay. Fine. It's a little early in his career to be changing lanes, but let me see what he's up to.* When he came over to the studio to see me, he sat down at the piano and proceeded to play a string of incredible pop songs. He played for half an hour without stopping, and there wasn't a whisper of jazz in any of it, but he hadn't lost the musicality that I had loved about him when I first heard him. Still, the change surprised me. I guess Peter woke up one morning and decided he wasn't going to be a jazz musician anymore. But he was still a phenomenal musician, and I wanted to work with him, and the feeling was mutual, apparently—but he wanted me to come to New York. "I need to do this in New York, David," he said. "This is my home. My band's here. This is where I'm comfortable."

"Well, I'm comfortable *here*," I said. "This is my home. And I hate New York. It's full of tall buildings and *elevators*." But of course I finally caved in. I said, "Okay, you win. I went to New York for Michael Jackson, so I guess I can do it for you." And I flew out with my programmer, Jochem vanderSaag, and with Humberto, and we made the album.

That's how that happened. My boss had opened that door. And it's funny because back in 1999, when Whalley became chairman of Warner Bros. Records, he brought me over from Atlantic and we got off to a rocky start. He was such a micromanager that I had difficulty with him from the beginning. I didn't really know how to be a company man, so I went around bad-rapping him a little—"He's a micromanager! I can't pin him down on anything! I can't get him to say yes to a single artist!"—and he got wind of this and called me into his office. I thought I was in for some heavy-duty praise—Groban was really beginning to take off—but instead he said, "Look, I gotta run this past you. I'm the chairman of the company, and you have to have my back. Period. If you don't have my back, you gotta leave."

I was stunned, but only for about ten seconds. Because it was really a great moment. It was clean and honest. And ever since that day I realized that when you work with someone, or for someone, you've got to have that person's back. It's really that simple. And to this day I make it a point to have the back of any person I'm in business with, even if we have our differences, and sometimes *more* so if we have differences, and it has served me very well. I learned a lot from Tom. He was running a tight ship seven years ago, and I suspect he knew that the music business was in for tough times, and to this day I think of him as an extraordinary executive and a visionary.

The other element in my life is charity work, of course, my own David Foster Foundation, which operates exclusively in Canada, and the dozens of organizations in this country to which I have lent, and will continue to lend, my musical skills. I don't do it to be a good Samaritan; I do it to feed my soul. Plus it's nice to perform without having to worry about filling the seats.

Just a few months ago, as I began writing this book, I had an opportunity to reconnect with Katie Luxton, a Canadian girl who received a heart transplant when she was seven—twenty years ago. The Luxtons were among the first families the foundation was able to help, and while I love making music, this is on a different plane entirely. Katie is adorable and beautiful and I'm sure she makes lots of hearts beat very fast.

In those early years, the foundation was headquartered in Victoria, and our fundraising efforts were limited to the home province, British Columbia. But when I decided that I wanted to go nationwide, I asked Mike Ravenhill, who had been with us from the beginning, to become our president—and I credit him with the successful expansion of the program.

There are many people who have devoted themselves tirelessly—and most of them without pay—to make the dream come true, including Lynn Mozley, the foundation's executive director, Chris Earthy, my best friend from childhood, Walter Creed, Hugh Curtis, Ian Tostenson (who took over as president in 2007), Dr. James Popkin, Derek Sturko, and Norm Kilarski—along with hundreds of other selfless volunteers. These are the people who really make it happen, but somehow I'm the one who ends up being unfairly glorified.

When we decided to broaden the foundation's reach, we kickstarted things with a big fundraiser in Vancouver, at the River Rock Casino, who proved to be our incredibly generous hosts, and followed that up with events in Calgary, Toronto, and Halifax. This year we are going to Edmonton, and we hope to raise three million dollars. And of course I always enlist my friends. In Vancouver, I had Clay Aiken, Bublé, and Babyface, and at the fundraiser in Niagara Falls I had Bublé again, along with Bocelli, Paul Anka, and Katherine McPhee.

When I got back from Niagara Falls, my friend Steve Wynn called. Wynn, the casino resort developer, is often credited with putting the flash back into Las Vegas. His company refurbished the Golden Nugget, the Mirage, Treasure Island, the Bellagio, and, of course, the Wynn. "I have a theater here at the Wynn and I really want to put something great in it," he said. "Would you think about some musical ideas for me?"

"Sure," I said. "It would be a pleasure."

After I got off the phone, I realized that my batting average wasn't that good with Wynn. Years earlier, I had taken him to see *Riverdance,* in Ireland, and he had passed. And more recently I had turned him on to Michael Bublé, but it was early in Michael's career and Steve wasn't sure he was big enough. Within a few years, however, with Bublé's star rising, he called to see if Bublé might have an appetite for Vegas, but by that time the ship had sailed.

No matter. I'd find something for him. I'd knock this one out of the park. So I started thinking about what we could do together, because I'm always hungry, always pitching. (Once you lose that hunger, it's over.) It occurred to me that I wouldn't mind being up on that stage at the Wynn, performing, and I came up with what I thought was a brilliant idea. I picked up the phone and called him back. "Steve," I said. "I think I've got the greatest idea on the planet and I want to come to Vegas to pitch it."

"Great!" he said.

A couple of weeks later, I flew out with Marc Johnston, a very savvy guy with an extensive knowledge of the music business, whom I'd met through Bocelli, when Marc was still working for Universal. I was impressed by the way Marc handled all the complicated details of Bocelli's life, and I enlisted him to help me with the non-producing parts of my career, so off we went to see Steve Wynn.

Steve was waiting for us in his sumptuous office. He had two executives with him, and after a little small talk he cut to the chase. "So," he said. "What's your idea?"

"Well," I said, "*American Idol* is the biggest show on television right now, and I think we should do '*American Idol* Live' in your theater." He didn't look particularly impressed, but I soldiered on. "We'll do it every weekend. At the end of five weeks, the winner will go home with $10,000. We'll keep going—we'll do five five-week rounds—and the next person will win $100,000. And at the end of the year the big winner will get a million dollars and a recording contract with me."

He still wasn't impressed—I could see the wheels in his head had come to a crashing halt—and I tried desperately to hype the show. "We could have betting, right at the seats! People could bet on the singers like they do at the horse races—go for the trifecta or whatever. And think of all the young people we'd get, all the people who love Vegas and want to get into show business." But this thing was dead. I could see that. I stopped talking.

"David," Steve said at last, "that's the worst idea I ever heard. If you can get anybody on the Strip, or *off* the Strip, to back that idea, I will personally kiss your ass."

I don't think my good friend Steve liked the idea, but I still love the guy. Genius is an overused word, but not on Steve Wynn.

When I returned to Los Angeles, a number of people began to talk to me about producing a PBS special of my own. I had helped produce PBS specials for Josh Groban, Michael Bublé, and Andrea Bocelli, and everyone seemed to think it was my turn. My fans included Marc Johnston, who pretty much spearheaded the whole thing; PBS network director David Horn; Bruce Gelb, who ran promotion for the show; and Cary Krukowski, who is part of the Boeddeker family, our Lake Las Vegas hosts. It took some convincing—I knew how much work it would entail—but in May 2008 we put together the concert, *David Foster and Friends*.

Marc Johnston offered to help me produce, and it became the usual nightmare. We had to change the date three times because of scheduling conflicts, but that never surprises me: It's hard enough to get my daughters to come to my house for dinner on any given Sunday, so you can imagine what it's like when you're dealing with busy superstars. And of course most of these people are also fans of private air travel—just like me—and one of the first things they want to know is if we're going to "supply the wings."

Among the first to commit were Groban, Bublé, and Bocelli, and in short order other artists signed on: Katherine McPhee, Boz Scaggs, Peter Cetera, Kenneth "Babyface" Edmonds, et al. I also got Charice Pempengco, an astonishing 16-year-old Philippine girl who was discovered on YouTube by one of Oprah Winfrey's producers.

As I've said before, a tribute concert is like a memorial while you're still alive, and—since I was alive—I had to hit the phones in earnest. (It's all about the Rolodex!) Then one morning I looked in the mirror and didn't like what I saw. I was going to be on national television, and I didn't look my best.

Fortunately, vanity is a great motivator. I worked out every day and managed to lose twenty pounds in three months. I cut out bread, pasta, butter, and desserts, with only minimal cheating, and I hit the gym five times a week with my trainer, Courtney Michaels. By the time we filmed the show, in May 2008, I was in better shape than I'd been in years, and I pretty much stuck to the regimen.

It's a good thing, too. Some twenty years ago, when I was in my mid-thirties, my friend and doctor, Josh Trabulus, figured out that my heart murmur was more than just a heart murmur. I went to see a specialist, and he broke the bad news: "You know, David, you have a bicuspid aortic valve. Before you're sixty, you're probably going to need a valve replacement." He explained that the valve is supposed to look a little like the Mercedes Benz emblem from the top, three flaps opening and closing. But I only have two flaps, and they were collapsing.

I was thirty-five when I got this news, and I thought, *Shit, I won't do anything. By the time I'm sixty they're gonna have a pill for that.* But here I am, almost fifty-nine, and there's no pill in sight. So every six months I confer with my medical team, headed by my brilliant Cedars-Sinai cardiologist, P. K. Shah, and they take a look at my heart—and each time the valve is a little closer to collapsing. At this point it's a waiting game. They're monitoring me closely, and the surgery is inevitable.

We've talked about my choices, of course. You can get a valve from a cadaver, a pig valve, or a plastic valve, and—to quote my first ex-wife—"I'll go with the cadaver." Pig is fine, I guess, but the plastic one doesn't interest me: It lasts forever, but it makes this sort of wheeze-and-click noise that seems to drive a lot of people nuts. You're trying to go to sleep at night and your heart refuses to shut up, which is the good news *and* the bad news, I guess.

And what if the beat isn't musical enough for me?

I'm not trying to make light of this, mind you. It's more than a little scary. They do have to crack your chest open. I just love doctors who say, "It's routine surgery." To which I always reply, "Maybe for *you.*"

I've been told that there's a one in 400 chance I won't wake up. Those seem like pretty good odds, but I still don't like them. On the other hand, I want to get it over with, and I want to be in the best possible physical shape so that I can zip through my recovery. That's why I'm still working out every day. Vanity's part of it, sure, but I want to be strong enough to handle the surgery.

By the way, there's also one other risk. During the surgery, you're hooked to one of those heart-lung machines for about five hours, and apparently the experience can erase up to a decade of your memory.

Upon hearing this, I asked my doctor, "Can I pick which decade?"

When we finally taped my PBS special, Andre Agassi, no stranger to charity, made a gracious opening speech, ending with: "All of us know that when you call David to ask for his help, before you finish asking he's already said yes." I guess *everybody* knows I can't say no.

A few people couldn't attend, and they sent videos. These included Kevin Costner, Whitney Houston, and Barbra Streisand, and their contributions aired throughout the evening.

Celine Dion wanted to come, but by the time we settled on a date she had committed to a fourteen-month world tour, so she suggested I come visit her on her turf, in Las Vegas, before her trip, and that we film the reunion for later use in the tribute. Eight months before my show, while she was still at Caesar's, I went to see her on her set. I didn't know how she was going to introduce me, but I knew it was complicated. Everything in her spectacular show is choreographed to within an inch of its life—there are a hundred moving parts—and she can't wander from the script, so I was flattered to just be there.

I was waiting in the wings for my cue, waiting for the applause to die down, and when the huge room fell silent Celine plunged in without further ado: "Tonight I am going to do something that I have never done in the four years that I have been on this stage," she said. "Many of my songs, songs like 'The Power of Love,' 'All by Myself,' 'When I Fall in Love,' 'All the Way,' 'Because You Loved Me,' 'Tell Him,' 'The Prayer,' 'To Love You More,' 'I Surrender'—and that's just to name a few—were produced by a good friend of mine. Ladies and gentlemen, please welcome a man that has been with me since he saw me sing in a tent in Québec twenty years ago; ladies and gentlemen, David Foster."

Wow. What an introduction!

She continued as I joined her on stage: "David, I have to say that I didn't believe you when one day you told me I was going to sing with Barbra Streisand, my idol, and it came true because of you. And I wanted to take this opportunity tonight to thank you for everything that you've done for me—in my life, in my career. What a thrill it is for me to have sung so many of the songs that you have produced for me and written for me."

Thrill for her? It was a thrill for me. I thought back to the very first day I had her in my Malibu studio, when I kept her waiting while my engineer and I went off to hit tennis balls on my newly surfaced tennis court. Hmm.

We did a couple of songs together, and I thanked her, and for days on end I couldn't stop thinking about her generosity. Not only did she break precedent that night by asking me to share the stage with her, but over the years she has taken time out from her hectic schedule on more than a dozen occasions, for no money, to help me with my charity work. And now that I think about it, almost every artist I've worked with has done exactly the same, *for no money*. And when you consider that it's not unusual for them to be offered a million dollars to sing half a dozen songs at a private party, that's incredibly generous—and a real testament to their character.

In November of last year, I went to New York for the launch of Andrea Bocelli's television special, and several of my friends decided to take advantage of the event to celebrate my birthday—my fifty-eighth. Before the party, everyone met at the Ziegfeld Theatre, to screen Bocelli's special, then we walked around the corner to the Bon Appetit Supper Club, on 57th Street. It used to be the home of the Hard Rock Café, and it had been redesigned as a temporary restaurant—I think they used it to film several episodes of *Iron Chef,* the cooking show. In fact, one of the Iron Chefs—Cat Cora, the only female in the bunch— actually cooked for us that night.

I heard the food was exceptional, but I didn't eat much because I spent most of the night on stage. I played with Bocelli, with Neil Sedaka, and with various other artists, and from time to time I'd tear myself away from the piano to mingle with the guests. Edgar Bronfman was there with his wife, as was Doug Morris and his wife. Katie Couric came with her boyfriend. Oprah's friend, Gayle King, also attended. And two of my daughters were there with Yolanda.

My friend Bill Haber, the Broadway producer, and one of the biggest spenders in theater, also stopped by, and at one point he got me alone in a corner. "I've been talking to Marc Johnston," he said, "and he seems to think you might be interested in writing a Broadway musical. Are you?"

"Absolutely," I said.

The next day, Haber and I met for lunch, and he pitched me an idea for a project, but I didn't respond to it. Then he told me he had another project he'd been wrestling with for seven years. "It's very frustrating," he said. "I've already been though two composers, and neither of them delivered."

He told me the idea and I liked it immediately, and when I returned to L.A. he sent me the fifteen-page synopsis and asked me if I could write two songs for him by the end of June. I looked at the synopsis, and I liked what I saw, but I was busy and didn't get around to composing the sample songs. One time he came to Los Angeles and we had dinner, and he asked me how it was going. I said I was still thinking about it. A month later, he sent me a blunt, four-word e-mail: "Time is running out."

Two weeks later, he called. "Have you got anything yet?" he asked.

"Not yet," I said. "But I'm working on it." Though of course I wasn't working on it at all.

Finally, June rolled around and three days before the deadline I sat in front at my piano and said, "Fuck it. I'm going to nail this." And instead of writing two songs for him I wrote four in one day. I demo'd them the next day, and I fired them off the day after that, and Haber listened to them immediately and called to say he loved them, and suddenly we were talking about moving forward. It felt great. It actually looked like I might be working on a Broadway musical. And it's funny, because I didn't think much of Broadway musicals during my session days, but a few years later, as you might recall, I actually began trying to get a musical off the ground with my friend Art Janov. That one is still floundering, and I now think of it as my *Malibu* musical. But Haber is convinced we're going to be on Broadway in 2010.

I feel like the luckiest guy on the planet. When I was in the throes of my third divorce, I thought I had made a terrible mess of my life, but I was wrong. Work is going incredibly well, and, more important, my daughters and I have grown closer than ever. And you know, as I watched them turn into beautiful young women, I did one of the smartest things I have ever done as a parent: I put a clause in my will stating that if they married before the age of twenty-five they wouldn't be entitled to any of my money. I did this to protect them from bad choices. I don't think that a twenty-two-year-old is sensible enough to make a decision about the person with whom she hopes to spend the rest of her life, and I want them to really think about it before making that kind of commitment. I also figured that if they fell in love at twenty-two they could hold on for another three years, at which point they'd be more ready. It's interesting, because you always hear about fathers who say they're going to reach for the shotgun the minute their daughters turn sixteen, and clearly they just don't get it. Bad news, guys: Your daughters are going to have sex. The sooner you come to terms with that, the better. What you really need to be worrying about is this whole marriage business, because a kid of nineteen or twenty or twenty-one is not ready to make a lifelong commitment to another human being. They don't know who they're supposed to marry, or why they should marry, or even *if* they should marry, and you need to help them understand that. Your kids will thank you for it, and they will be much happier as a result. Right now, all my kids are happy. And since—as I've said—I'm only as happy as my saddest child, I'm pretty damn happy right now, too. I know I owe a great deal to my ex-wife, Rebecca, an amazing mother to three of my five girls, but I'd like to think that maybe I did a few things right as a father, too.

I wasn't the greatest dad around, certainly, not by a long shot, and it still gnaws at me, but sometimes something happens that makes me think I wasn't a complete failure. Last Father's Day I got an e-mail from Rebecca: "These Hallmark holidays have gotten crazy with pressure to purchase ridiculous gadgets or over-the-top high-end must-haves. What I want to give you is my thanks for being the father to our girls. Through it all you have never wavered in your love and devotion to your children. No matter how deeply immersed in the music you were, you'd always take their phone calls, always call to find out where they were, confirming that they were safe. You stalked them, but on that rare day that you didn't, they missed you hunting them down. You loved them hard, you loved them fairly. I honor you today, love you for the great dad you are. May today be all you want it to be."

I think she was being too generous, but I was very moved by the letter. I am still working on becoming a better father and a better man, and I will never stop trying.

I try to be a good brother, too. Four of my sisters live in British Columbia. Ruth is a registered nurse and has spent twenty-five years working with cancer patients, unimaginably heart-wrenching work. She is the Florence Nightingale in the family—the one all of us go to for medical advice—and she seems to know more than most doctors. She's married and has three kids. My other sister, Jeanie, trained as a practical nurse, and is known for her wit and ambush humor. (She always makes me laugh.) She's actually married to Ruth's husband's brother. She has three great kids, too, so those six kids are double cousins.

My third sister, Maureen, was always the adventurous one—like my daughter Jordan—and was racing cars at sixteen, then spent thirty years managing a construction company. She has since slowed down and is married to Marty, another great guy. They have no children, and for the past few years they've been driving around Canada in an RV, enjoying the open road. I have one more sister in B.C., Barbara. She is a bit of a loner, and doesn't often reach out to us, but she is smart and creative and so full of good ideas that I wish she'd try her hand as a film or television producer.

My other two sisters live in Los Angeles, and both of them are in the music business. Marylou remains married to Ian Eales, the guy who saved Jay Graydon's life with a well-timed Heimlich maneuver, and she has been the music coordinator on a lot of big Hollywood films. Sometimes I meet big Hollywood players and the only reason I get props is because I'm her brother. It's the same with my sister Jaymes. She worked for Warners for a long time, and for the past decade has been working with me. She has a knack for finding talent before it hits. She has also been in the news recently because she just had her first child with Clay Aiken, of *American Idol* fame. She and Clay are best friends. She was producing music for him, and they have now produced a child together—Parker Foster Aiken, DOB 08–08–08, at 8:08 a.m. (believe it or not)—and I applaud it. She was married for twenty-three years, and after the marriage ended she realized she wanted children, so she had one.

What could be more perfect?

When I think about my family, I often wonder if they know how much their unconditional support has meant to me over the years. I was the middle of seven children, and you'd think I'd have gotten lost in there, but all my sisters took great care of me. And after I went off and started making my way in the music world, they never wavered in their support, were never jealous of my achievements, and never asked anything of me in return. It doesn't get much better than that.

When I was writing this book, I didn't realize it was going to force me to become so introspective. I've always said that I'm not interested in seeing a shrink because I don't want to dig that deep: I'm afraid of what I might find. And in some ways, that still holds. I wake up on Mondays, Wednesdays, and Fridays and think that, musically speaking, I'm the greatest thing on the planet. But on Tuesdays, Thursdays, and Saturdays I wake up thinking I'm a fraud and a failure, and I can't figure out how I got this far without being found out. On Sundays I don't think about any of it. That's the honest truth; that's as deep as it gets.

But in these pages, reviewing my life, I was forced to dig a little deeper, and I found myself wondering who I was without the music. And I really don't know how to answer that. I *am* the music. I've been the music since the day I was five years old and sat down for my very first piano lesson. Without the music, I wouldn't have had this amazing life.

And in fact, some months ago, just before the PBS special, a reporter said to me: "I believe if you hadn't been born, pop music would sound different today." Hmm. It would be nice to think that in some small way I *have* had an effect on music. And maybe I have. I don't know. I do know that I am often approached by musicians and songwriters, young and old, black and white, and that they invariably have the same thing to say: *I love your music. I don't play that type of music, mind you, but I was heavily influenced by it, and it is very much a part of what I've become.* I hear that a lot, and I never get tired of it—so maybe that reporter was right: Maybe the David Foster Sound will rate a footnote or two in the history books. I hope so.

There is one misconception about me, however, that I'd like to clear up, and it's this: I do *not* create careers. I have helped put a number of very talented people on the map, certainly—Celine Dion, Josh Groban, Michael Bublé, to name just three—and in the months and years ahead I hope I'll be adding plenty of names to the list. But I'm not a star-maker; I'm a hit-maker. That's what I'm good at—hits—and that's what it's all about for me. And it seems to work. As another reporter told me recently, "David, I don't believe there is an independent producer on the planet who has sold as many records as you have. Is that true?"

And I said, "I don't know, but it sounds right, and it sounds good—and I'll take it."

Still, as I've said, I've lived my entire creative life feeling as if I'm never going to produce another hit. That sensation is very real. My latest hit always feels like my last: *I'll never pull it off again.* And there's no rhyme or reason for it. I wonder where that feeling comes from, and I'm sure I could find out in therapy—but I've always told my friends that I'd like to reach my eighty-fifth birthday without subjecting myself to self-analysis, and that's still the plan. And I don't need analysis, anyway. I'd like to think I'm a better person now than I was twenty years ago; a better father; a better friend; a better mate; a better musician; a better producer. I'm not there yet, certainly, but on good days I actually think I'm moving in the right direction.

And I've got to say it: There are fifteen Grammys sitting on my piano, along with an Emmy and a Golden Globe. I like that. I like looking at them. I think they'd look better if they shared that crowded space with a Tony and an Oscar (nominated three times, lost three times), but on Mondays, Wednesdays, and Fridays I think that maybe that'll happen, too. That's the goal, anyway. You've got to stay hungry to succeed.

Hunger. That's a huge part of the equation. I am often invited to speak to classes, at UCLA or USC or wherever, and I love it, but I am always troubled by the fact that the kids invariably start with the same question: *How do I make it as a musician/manager/producer?*

I've learned how to stop that, though, from the very first moment I step up to the podium: "Anybody in this class who puts up his or her hand up to ask me how to become a record producer is never going to become a record producer," I say. "Because if you have to ask, you don't have what it takes—and it's not going to happen."

I then look at that sea of young faces and they're not moving, not breathing; that's the one question they *all* wanted to ask. And I tell them: "I never asked how to be a record producer. It happened by osmosis. It happened by the moves I made. You could be the guy sweeping the studio floor, but if you do your job well someone is going to notice. And one day that someone is going to turn to you and say, 'We've had a cancellation. There's no one on the board between two and four. I know you want to make a demo, so go ahead and make your demo.'"

Then I ask the class, "How many singers do we have here?" And I'll get maybe ten hands. "How many bass players?" Four hands. "How many guitar players?" Twenty hands. "How many people here want to produce?" Three hands. And then I say, "Look around. There are 300 of you right in this room. Everything you need to make it happen is right here, in front of you, and you're not seeing it. That young lady wants to be a producer. That guy with the mohawk wants to play bass. This kid in the front row has a daddy who is going to buy him his own recording studio. That guy wants to manage, and the girl next to him wants to be an agent, and those two, three, four, five guys play guitar.

"Quincy Jones used to say: 'You want a hit, there are three important ingredients: One, the song; two, the song. And three, the song.'

"I'll add one more to that," I tell the class. "Networking. Stop listening to me and start exchanging phone numbers. Stop asking people how to make it happen. Just *make* it happen. *You* have to do it, not me and not anyone else. And in your hearts you all know what it takes: hard work. It's as simple as that. Hard fucking work."

I tell them that they have to live, eat, and breathe music, 24/7, and that even then the chances of making it are slim. They need to put blinders on and think of absolutely nothing else. They have to have a goal, and they have to move directly toward that goal—in a straight, undistracted line. Anything less than that—well, it's not going to happen.

Take it from Abraham Lincoln: "Things may come to those who wait . . . but only the things left behind by those who hustle." (If you don't believe he said that, look it up!)

You cannot take your eye off the tiger, I tell them. If you do, you're making room for somebody else. It is tough to break in and even tougher to *stay* in. In fact, the only thing harder than getting your first hit record is getting your second one. (I'm living proof of that.) If you don't understand that, you're simply not going to succeed. But if you do, it sure as hell is worth it! I have spent more than forty years in the music business, and it is a privilege and an honor to be part of it. And I would never abuse that privilege. I won't go on drinking binges. I won't snort cocaine. I won't get high on dope that makes me want to sleep all day. And I'm not going to take Saturdays off because if I do somebody else won't. And *nobody* is going to take my place. That's why I work every Saturday, because I'm not going to move over for anyone.

I love this business. I am tired of hearing people complain about it. When Elvis came along, people said good music was gone forever. The Beatles came along, same thing. "The new generation is here, and music has gone to hell." Punk, disco, rap—the only constant is change. And that's a good thing. People who tell you they got out of the business because music got bad are lying to you and to themselves. They didn't leave the music business. The music business left them. Don't be that person.

I'm often asked, "If there was one thing you could change about your life, what would it be?" And I always say the same thing, "I wouldn't change a fucking thing." That's right. I love my life. I love my family. I love my friends. I love my work. I love making hits. I love music.

And I wouldn't change a thing.

Acknowledgments

Whe n I finally decided to write this book, there were a few things I couldn't get my head around: One, did anybody really give a shit about my story or what I had to say? Two, in trying to be as truthful as possible, would I alienate certain people? And three—and most important—how was I possibly going to include everyone I wanted to include?

On this last issue, there are hundreds of people who mean a lot to me, many of whom have been a critical part of my journey, and I apologize in advance if you didn't get a shout-out. I know how it is: Whenever a guy like me writes a book, all of his friends rush to the local bookstore and immediately turn to the index, looking for their own names. And I know this because I've done it myself. So if you're not in there, I apologize. But I'd also like to take this opportunity to speak to some of you directly . . .

Thanks to Bob Daley and Terry Semel, the two guiding lights who brilliantly ran Warner Bros. Pictures for so many years, and who subsequently became my bosses when they took over Warner Music. Thanks also to their terrific wives, Jane Semel and Carole Bayer Sager. I still remember when it came time to renew my deal, and Terry—

knowing I was a total jet-slut—said the magic words: "Not only *can* you use the Warners jet, I WANT you to use it." Thank you. That really clinched it.

Thanks to Ned Shankman and his partner, Ron DeBlasio. Ned was my lawyer and then my manager, back in the eighties, and he made great deals for me and taught me a lot about the music business.

Thanks to Brian Avnet, whom I met when I was playing piano for the stage version of *The Rocky Horror Picture Show*—thirty-three years ago. Brian managed me in the nineties, and he manages Josh Groban, Renee Olstead, and my friend Eric Benet, an amazing singer.

Greetings to my long-time business manager, Ralph Goldman, now retired, who took me on when I was nobody, and who took my calls anytime, day and night. Ralph also saved me from my first business manager, who somehow never got around to paying my taxes. I remember meeting Ralph for the first time, for lunch at The Palm, in Beverly Hills, and I was very proud of myself because I had just saved one million dollars. And Ralph said, "Well, I've been reviewing your history, and I'm going to take you on as a client, and the first thing you need to do is give the U.S. government a million dollars in back taxes." I literally dropped my fork! I went from millionaire to pauper before I'd had my first bite!

Thanks to Howard Grossman, who took over as my business manager ten years ago, after Ralph retired. A friend, a confidant, and a guy I'm on the phone with every day, sometimes several times a day. You bring me peace of mind, man, and I appreciate it. I don't think there's anyone in my professional life that has my back the way you do.

Courtney Blooding: You started with me as an intern until I found out you could sing beautifully, run Pro Tools, book musicians, and knew a little something about the engineering end of the business, too. I couldn't function without you. A shout-out also to your fiancé, Patrick, one of the guys who stormed Saddam Hussein's palace early in the war. No one messes with us on Patrick's watch.

A special thanks to Kathy Frangetis, who began as my assistant at Warners twelve years ago and has been with me ever since. She's always dependable, never gets rattled, and she does a great job managing my calendar (despite the fact that I'm impossible to manage).

Hello to Joel Schumacher, who directed *St. Elmo's Fire,* and who broke my cherry when it came to doing film music. You are the best first guy a guy could have!

Rob Lowe, whom I met on that same movie—and who is a good friend to this day. Thanks for being in the *St. Elmo's* video, man—that was huge for me. And you're still so fucking good-looking that I should have put your face on the cover of this book, not mine. I still remember the time I had you playing sax at the home of Michael and Jenna King during that fundraiser for Bill Clinton. Everyone was astonished at your talent, unaware that the *real* sax player was right behind the curtain.

Hello to George Schlatter, the genius creator of *Laugh-In*. Still have fond memories of that Carousel of Hope Ball we did together for Barbara Davis—you know, the one where we were stuck recording Bocelli in a hotel room. I also love the way you always greet me with a megawatt smile.

Jackie Collins—love you, love your books. You're a real guy's woman. You like a good dirty joke once in a while, but you expect a gentleman to open your car door, too.

A million thanks to all the great engineers and programmers that have come through my camp: Neil Devor, Mic Guizoski (who mixed so many hits for me), Felipe Elgueta, Alex Rodriguez, Dave Reitzas, Bill Schnee, Al Schmitt, Ric Bowen, Simon Franglen, Bob Clearmountain, and Michael Bottiker—to name just a few. And thanks also to Jochem vanderSaag, who has helped me so much these past few years with his arranging, writing, programming, and—more recently—producing skills.

Then there's my good friend Humberto Gatica: We're like an old married couple. Together, apart, together, apart. But we sure made some great music together over these thirty-plus years, didn't we? You are a great engineer, mixer, and co-producer, and you have the best ears in the business.

Diane Warren—the great songwriter. You write it, I'll produce it. What a team. You're quirky and super talented. Great combination.

Richard Marx, who in the eighties showed up at the studio to watch me work, and ended up spending two years there with no pay. Then one day he told me, "I want to make my own album." And I said, "Richard, you have an amazing talent—I think you're going to be a very successful songwriter and producer—but you're not a singer." And fifty million albums later . . . Well, like I've admitted, when I screw up, I screw up big.

Hello to Fee Waybill, lead singer of the Tubes. What an amazing talent. I learned a lot from you, so thanks for letting me produce two of your albums.

Daryl Hall and John Oates. We clashed a bit, yeah, but we listened to one another, and good things happened.

A big hello to Donald Trump, smart as a whip, charismatic, and a great listener. I will never forget that Miss Universe Pageant, man: me, Quincy Jones, and Los Angeles Mayor Antonio Villaraigosa, sitting in the front row together, drooling like schoolboys.

Elton John: Think back to the mid-seventies, You were looking for a whole new sound. My friend Nigel Olsson, your great drummer, arranged a meeting, and I went over to your house in Beverly Hills, with my brother-in-law, Robbie, and found you puttering around the garden. "How much do you want per week to go on the road with me?" you asked. "Five grand," I replied. You shook my hand: "Thank you. This meeting is over." I still love you, man. No one has been able to sustain it quite like you have.

Hello to Jerry Moss, the very bright, calm, and talented co-founder of A&M Records, who called me into his office in the late seventies to see about having me on board, exclusively, as a staff producer. "What would it take?" he asked me. And I said, "Two million a year for three years." "Thank you for your time," he said. "Good luck out there." And of course I ran into him years later, and I refreshed his memory, and he said, "You didn't tell me you were going to become David Foster!!"

A warm thank you and a big hug to my friend Chris Earthy, who has been close to me since I was thirteen. I want you to know how important it has been for me to have had you in my life from the very beginning. We have always been there for each other. We are real friends. And you're *still* helping me with all my charity concerts . . . Chris had a stroke while I was working on this book, and I flew up to Vancouver to see him, and the man is recovering very nicely. In true Earthman fashion, he suggested a "Jokes for Strokes" charity. Life is precious. Too bad it takes such drastic incidents to remind us!

A big shout-out to that core group of world-class, super-talented musicians who always try to make themselves available to me— whether it's for a nonpaying charity gig, a concert in Japan, or a visit to my studio to help make my records that much better. Nathan East, Michael Thompson, Dean Parks, Randy Waldman, Greg Phillinganes, Neil Stubenhaus, J. R. Robinson, Vinnie Caluida, Jeremy Lubbock, Jerry Hey, and Bill Ross. You guys are the best of the best. If you surround yourself with killer talent—what a concept—it actually works!

Thanks to Lynn Mozley, executive director of the David Foster Foundation, and thanks especially to all the foundation's presidents: Brian Cooper, Hugh Curtis, Walter Creed, Jim Reger, Mike Ravenhill, and Ian Tostenson. A big thanks to the hundreds of volunteers who have given so selflessly of their time to help so many families.

And thanks to the 407 families I have met through the foundation. Helping you has helped me in ways you cannot imagine. Thank you for doing so much to enrich my life.

Thanks to my dear friends Barry and Jelinda DeVorzon, Layla and Essam Khashoggi, Bob and Tamour Manoukian, Jimmy and Sara Argoroplis, Ray and Ghada Irani, Barbara Davis, Charles and Danica Perez, Arnold and Anne Kopelson, and a special shout-out to Haim and Cheryl Saban.

Hello to my friend Norm Pattiz, a generous, no-bullshit guy who hit big with the Westwood One Radio Network, and to his wife, Mary. I'm always available for a floor seat at the Staples Center during a Lakers game. You have my number!

Ryan Seacrest—the hardest working man in showbiz, and what a talent! You are going to own the world some day. You are the next Dick Clark.

Phil Anschultz, one of the all-time great entrepreneurs. Among his many accomplishments, he started the Foundation for a Better Life— using his money to make the world a better place. And hello also to Garry Dixon, president of that spectacular organization, for being another one of the good guys.

Mike Milken, Larry Ellison, and Craig McCaw, who are fascinating not because they're rich, but because they figured out how to become rich—and then used their wealth to do good things.

A shout-out to Dennis and Phyllis Washington, who always come to my foundation events, and who donated 100,000 acres of land to create a utopia for underprivileged kids. And thanks to Walter and Sue Scott, for their selflessness and generosity.

To Jerry Perenchio and Kirk Kerkorian, thanks for doing so much for so many, and for always doing it under the radar. No credit, no headlines, no glory—giving the way the Kabbalah tells us to give.

To Bill Gates and Tim Blixseth, thanks for hanging around the piano and singing songs with me on that memorable night. Let's do it again. And Tim, you know we're living each other's lives. I'm glad we've become such good friends.

Mo Ostin, who built Warner Bros. Records into a monolith, and who at eighty years of age is still going strong. I still remember that boat trip we went on, and how excited I was at the thought that I was going to spend an entire week at the master's feet, learning everything there was to know about showbiz. And I still remember your remark: "I honestly don't know how I do it. If I did, I'd tell you, but it's a mystery—even to me."

Thanks to all my aunts and uncles and cousins—the Fosters and the Vantreights. And to our wonderful neighbors on Ascot Drive, where I grew up.

Thanks, finally, to Pablo Fenjves, who started out as my collaborator on this project, proved to be a wonderful co-writer, and became a friend; to Jan Miller, who had to convince me—on more than one occasion—that I really needed to write this book; and to Marc Johnston, who shared Jan's enthusiasm for the book and various new, out-of-the-box endeavors.

In closing, I'd like to say a few more words about family, starting with my six wonderful sisters. If I had a perfect childhood, and I think I did, it was thanks largely to all of you. Without your unconditional support—then and now—I'm not sure I would have made it. Everyone should be lucky enough to have a Ruth, Jeanie, Maureen, Marylou, Barbara, and Jaymes in his or her life.

So there you have it. I realize this part of the book is only interesting to those who are mentioned in it, but it's also important to me and . . . well . . . it's *my* book. I'm sure I've left out a shitload of important stuff, but—on a final note—a few more words about my children and my family.

I understand that this book is not, nor should it be, about my children or my sisters. But the thing is, if I were reading this, I couldn't help but wonder *Where are his children? What are they up to? What schools are they going to? What are their grades like? Where did they go on family trips? What are they doing with their lives? Who are their boyfriends? What music do they listen to? Do they like their dad's music?* etc.

The truth is, for most of my life I put my work first and my family second—three divorces, big surprise!—and the book reflects that. But I've been making up for lost time. And if, as I've said, you're only as happy as your happiest child, at the moment I'm a ten.

Nothing gives me more joy than seeing my kids happy and doing well—it's really the only important thing left to me now. Getting older is shitty for only one reason: The body can't do what it did when you were twenty, thirty, or even fifty. In fact, life is a circle. You start out with no hair, no mind, no coordination, in diapers, and—if you live long enough—you end up the same way. But everything else about getting old is fantastic. And my old-age pension is coming up in six years. And that's certainly worth sticking around for!

Grammy® Awards Nominations and Wins

1979

1. Song of the Year: "After the Love Has Gone" (Earth, Wind & Fire), David Foster, Jay Graydon, Bill Champlin
2. **Best Rhythm & Blues Song: "After the Love Has Gone" (Earth, Wind & Fire), David Foster, Jay Graydon, Bill Champlin**
3. Best Arrangement Accompanying Vocalist(s): "After the Love Has Gone" (Earth, Wind & Fire), David Foster and Jerry Hey

1980

4. Best Album of Original Score Written for a Motion Picture: *Urban Cowboy* (David Foster produced Boz Scaggs's "Love Look What You've Done To Me"

1982

5. **Best Cast Show Album: *Dreamgirls*, Henry Krieger (Composer), Tom Eyen (Lyricist), David Foster (Producer)**
6. Producer of the Year (Non-Classical): David Foster

1983

7. Best Instrumental Arrangement Accompanying Vocals: "Mornin' " (Al Jarreau), David Foster, Jay Graydon, Jeremy Lubbock

1984

8. Record of the Year: "Hard Habit to Break" (Chicago), David Foster, Producer
9. **Best Instrumental Arrangement Accompanying Vocals: "Hard Habit to Break" (Chicago), David Foster & Jeremy Lubbock**
10. Best Vocal Arrangement for Two or More Voices: "Hard Habit to Break" (Chicago), David Foster, Peter Cetera
11. Best Vocal Arrangement for Two or More Voices: "What About Me?" (Kenny Rogers, Kim Carnes, James Ingram), David Foster
12. Best Album of Original Score Written for a Motion Picture: *Ghostbusters* (Various Artists)
13. **Producer of the Year (Non-Classical): David Foster**

1985

14. Album of the Year: *We Are the World* (Various Artists)
15. Best Pop Instrumental Performance: "Love Theme from *St. Elmo's Fire*," David Foster
16. Best Rhythm & Blues Song: "Through the Fire" (Chaka Khan), David Foster, Tom Keane, Cynthia Weil
17. Best Instrumental Composition: "Love Theme from *St. Elmo's Fire*," David Foster

18. Best Album of Original Score Written for a Motion Picture: *St. Elmo's Fire* (David Foster and Others)
19. Best Instrumental Arrangement Accompanying Vocals: "Through the Fire" (Chaka Khan), David Foster
20. Producer of the Year (Non-Classical): David Foster

1986

21. Best Pop Instrumental Performance: David Foster (David Foster)
22. **Best Instrumental Arrangement Accompanying Vocals: "Somewhere" (Barbra Streisand), David Foster**
23. Producer of the Year (Non-Classical): David Foster

1988

24. Best Instrumental Composition: "Winter Games" (David Foster)
25. Best Performance Music Video: "The Symphony Sessions" (David Foster)

1991

26. **Record of the Year: "Unforgettable" (Natalie Cole and Nat King Cole), David Foster, Producer**
27. **Album of the Year: *Unforgettable* (Natalie Cole), Natalie Cole, Andre Fisher, David Foster, Tommy Lipuma**
28. **Producer of the Year (Non-Classical): David Foster**

1993

29. **Record of the Year: "I Will Always Love You" (Whitney Houston), David Foster, Producer**
30. **Album of the Year: *The Bodyguard (Original Soundtrack Album)* (Various Artists)**
31. Best Song Written Specifically for Motion Picture or TV: "I Have Nothing" (Whitney Houston), David Foster, Linda Thompson
32. **Best Instrumental Arrangement Accompanying Vocals: "When I Fall in Love (From *Sleepless In Seattle*)" (Celine Dion and Clive Griffin), David Foster, Jeremy Lubbock**
33. Best Instrumental Arrangement Accompanying Vocals: "I Have Nothing" (Whitney Houston), David Foster, William Ross
34. Best Instrumental Arrangement Accompanying Vocals: "Some Enchanted Evening" (Barbra Streisand), David Foster, Johnny Mandel
35. **Producer of the Year (Non-Classical): David Foster**

1995

36. Album of the Year: *HIStory Past, Present & Future Book I* (Michael Jackson and Various Artists)

1996

37. Record of the Year: "Because You Loved Me (Theme from *Up Close and Personal*)," Celine Dion, David Foster, Producer
38. **Album of the Year: *Falling Into You,* (Celine Dion and Various Artists)**

39. Best Instrumental Arrangement with Accompanying Vocal(s): "When I Fall in Love" (Natalie Cole and Nat King Cole), David Foster, Alan Broadbent

40. Producer of the Year (Non-Classical): David Foster

1999

41. Best Instrumental Arrangement Accompanying Vocals: "The Prayer" (Celine Dion and Andrea Bocelli), David Foster

2003

42. Best Instrumental Arrangement with Accompanying Vocal(s): "Summertime" (Renee Olstead), David Foster, John Clayton, Jr.

2004

43. Best Instrumental Arrangement with Accompanying Vocal(s): "Can't Buy Me Love" (Michael Bublé), David Foster, John Clayton, Jr.

2005

44. Best Traditional Pop Album: *It's Time* (Michael Bublé), David Foster and Humberto Gatica, Producers

2007

45. Best Traditional Pop Album: *Call Me Irresponsible* (Michael Bublé), David Foster and Humberto Gatica, Producers

Emmy® Awards Nominations and Win

Bold text indicates Emmy win.

1997

1. Oustanding Music & Lyrics: Centennial Olympic Games, Opening Ceremonies, Kenneth "Babyface" Edmonds (Composer), David Foster (Composer), Linda Thompson (Lyricist)

2003

2. **Oustanding Music & Lyrics: The Concert for World Children's Day, David Foster (Composer), Linda Thompson (Lyricist)**

2006

3. Oustanding Music Direction: Andrea Bocelli: *Amore Under the Desert Sky* (Great Performances), David Foster (Music Director)

Golden Globes® Nominations and Win

1987

1. Best Original Song—Motion Picture: "The Glory of Love," David Foster, Peter Cetera, and Diane Nini

1988

2. Best Original Song—Motion Picture: "The Secret of My Success," David Foster, Jack Blades, Tom Keane, and Michael Landau

1999

3. **Best Original Song—Motion Picture: "The Prayer," David Foster, Carole Bayer Sager, Tony Renis, and Alberto Testa**

Academy Awards® Nominations

1986 (59th)

Music (Original Song)—"Glory of Love" from *The Karate Kid, Part II*—Music by Peter Cetera and David Foster, Lyrics by Peter Cetera and Diane Nini

1992 (65th)

Music (Original Song)—"I Have Nothing" from *The Bodyguard*—Music by David Foster, Lyrics by Linda Thompson

1998 (71st)

Music (Original Song)—"The Prayer" from *The Quest for Camelot*—Music by David Foster and Carole Bayer Sager, Lyrics by Carole Bayer Sager, David Foster, Tony Renis, and Alberto Testa

Juno Awards Nominations and Wins

Bold text indicates Juno Awards win.

1985

Composer of the Year
Artist: David Foster

1985

Producer of the Year
Artist: David Foster
Title: *Chicago 17*
Performer: Chicago

1986

Composer of the Year
Artist: David Foster

1986

Instrumental Artist(s) of the Year
Artist: David Foster

1986

Producer of the Year
Artist: David Foster
Title: *St. Elmo's Fire* Soundtrack
Performer: Various Artists

1987

Composer of the Year
Artist: David Foster

1989

Composer of the Year
Artist: David Foster

1987

Instrumental Artist(s) of the Year
Artist: David Foster
Label: WEA

1989

Instrumental Artist(s) of the Year
Artist: David Foster
Label: WEA

1989

Producer of the Year
Artist: David Foster
Title: Winter Games
Performer: David Foster
Label: WEA

1991

Producer of the Year
Artist: David Foster
Title: "Have a Heart"; "Love by Another Name"
Performer: Celine Dion; Celine Dion
Label: Columbia; Columbia

1992

Instrumental Artist(s) of the Year
Artist: David Foster
Label: Atlantic

1995

Producer of the Year
Artist: David Foster
Title: "The Power of My Love"; "I Swear"
Performer: *The Colour of My Love,* Celine Dion;
    All-4-One, All-4-One
Label: Columbia/Sony; Atlantic/Warner

1996

Producer of the Year
Artist: David Foster (Co-producer Madonna)
Title: "You'll See"; "I Can Love You Like That"
Performer: *Something to Remember,* Madonna; *And
    the Music Speaks,* All-4-One
Label: Maverick/ Warner; Atlantic/Warner

1997

Producer of the Year
Artist: David Foster
Title: "Runaway"; "Both Sides Now"

Performer: The Corrs; Natalie Cole
Label: Atlantic/Warner; Rhino/Warner

1999

Best Producer
Artist: David Foster
Title: "I Never Loved You Anyway"; "Have You Ever?"
Performer: The Corrs; Brandy
Label: Atlantic/Warner; Atlantic/Warner

2005

Jack Richardson Producer of the Year
Artist: David Foster
Title: "You Raise Me Up"; "Can't Help Falling In Love"
Performer: *Closer*—Josh Groban; *Come Fly with
    Me*—Michael Bublé
Label: Reprise/Warner; Warner Bros./Warner

2006

Jack Richardson Producer of the Year
Artist: David Foster
Title: "Home," "Feeling Good"
Performer: *It's Time*—Michael Bublé
Label: 143/Reprise/Warner

2007

Jack Richardson Producer of the Year
Artist: David Foster
Title: "Un Giorno Per Noi (Romeo e Giulietta)"/
"Un Dia Llegara"
Performer: *Awake*—Josh Groban
Label: Reprise/Warner

Printed in the United States
By Bookmasters